We Moderns

Enigmas and Guesses

Edwin Muir and H. L. Mencken

CONTENTS

INTRODUCTION

        I.—THE OLD AGE,

        II.—ORIGINAL SIN,

        III.—WHAT IS MODERN?

        IV.—ART AND LITERATURE,

        V.—CREATIVE LOVE,

        VI.—THE TRAGIC VIEW.

INTRODUCTION

That a young Scotsman, reacting from the vast emotional assault of the late ferocious war, should have withdrawn himself into an ivory tower in Glasgow town, and there sat himself down in heroic calm to wrestle with the vexatious and no doubt intrinsically insoluble problems of being and becoming—this was surely nothing to cause, whispers among connoisseurs of philosophical passion, for that grim, persistent, cold-blooded concern with the fundamental mysteries of the world has been the habit of the Scots ever since they emerged from massacre and blue paint. From blue paint, indeed, the transition was almost instantaneous to blue souls, and the conscience of Britain, such as it is, has dwelt north of the Cheviot Hills ever since. Find a Scot, and you are at once beset by a metaphysician, or, at all events, by a theologian. But for a young man of those damp, desolate parts, throwing himself into the racial trance, to emerge with a set of ideas reaching back, through Nietzsche and even worse heretics, to the spacious, innocent, somewhat gaudy days of the Greek illumination—for such a fellow, so bred and circumscribed, to come out of his tower with a concept of life as a grand and glittering adventure, a tremendous spectacle, an overpowering ecstasy, almost an orgy—such a phenomenon was, and is, quite sufficient to lift the judicious eyebrow. Yet here is this Mr. Edwin Muir of Caledonia bearing just that outlandish contraband, offering just that strange flouting of all things traditionally Scotch. What he preaches in the ensuing aphorisms is the emancipation of the modern spirit from its rotting heritage of ingenuous fears and exploded certainties. What he denounces most bitterly is the abandonment of a world that is beautifully surprising and charming to the rule of sordid, timid and unimaginative men—the regimentation of ideas in a system that is half a denial of the obvious and half a conglomeration of outworn metaphors, all taken too literally. And what he pleads for most eloquently, with his cold, reserved northern eloquence, is the wholehearted acceptance of "life as a sacrament,... life as joy triumphing over fate,... life made innocent,... life washed free from how much filth of remorse, guilt, contempt, 'sin'."...

It goes without saying that the red hand of Nietzsche is in all this. The Naumburg Antichrist, damned for five years running by the indignation of all right-thinking men, has made steady and enormous progress under cover. There has never been a time, indeed, when his notions enjoyed a wider dispersion or were poll-parrotted unwittingly by greater numbers of the righteous. Excessive draughts of the democratic cure-all, swallowed label, cork, testimonials and all, have brought Christendom to bed with *Katzenjammer*—and there stands the seductive antidote in its leering blue bottles. Where would philosophical opponents of Bolshevism be without Nietzsche? Who would devise arguments for them, eloquence for them, phrases for them? On all sides one hears echoes of him often transformed from his harsh bass to a piping falsetto, but nevertheless recognizable enough. Any port in a storm! If God is asleep, then turn to the Devil! The show offers the best laughing that heathen have enjoyed, perhaps, since the Hundred Years' War. And there is an extra snicker in the fact that Scotland, once again, seems to resume the old trade of intellectual smuggling. If one Scot is to the front with so forthright a piece as "We Moderns," then surely there must be a thousand other Scots hard at it in a *pianissimo* manner. Thus, I suppose, the crime of Carlyle is repeated on a wholesale scale, and once again the poor Sassenach is inoculated with pathogenic Prussian organisms. On this side of the ocean the business is less efficiently organized; we have no race of illicit metaphysicians on our border. But the goods come in all the same. I have heard more prattling of stale Nietzscheism of late, from men bearing the flag in one hand and the cross in the other, than I ever heard in the old days from parlour anarchists and unfrocked priests. Nietzsche, belatedly discovered by a world beset by terrors too great for it and mysteries too profound, becomes almost respectable, nay, almost Episcopalian!

What ails it, at bottom, is the delusion that all the mysteries, given doctors enough, theories enough, pills enough, may be solved—that it is all a matter of finding a panacea, unearthing a prophet, passing a bill. If it turns to Nietzsche, however gingerly and suspiciously, it will turn only to fresh disappointment and dismay, for Nietzsche is no quack with another sure cure, but simply an iconoclast who shows that all the sure cures of the past and present have failed, and *must* fail—and particularly the sure cure of the mob, the scheme of determining the diagnosis by taking a vote, the notion that the medicine which most pleases the grossest palates is the medicine to get the patient upon his legs. Nietzsche is no reformer; he is an assassin of reformers; if he preaches anything at all, it is that reform is useless, illusory— above all, unnecessary. The patient is really not dying at all. Let him get up and dance! Let him pick up his bed and employ it upon the skulls of his physicians! Life is not a disease to be treated with boluses and philtres, not an affliction to be shirked and sentimentalized, but an adventure to be savoured and enjoyed—life, here and now, is the highest imaginable experience. What the world needs is not a cure for it, but room for it, freedom for it, innocent zest for it. So accepted and regarded, half of its terrors vanish at once, and even its unescapable catastrophes take on a certain high stateliness, a fine æsthetic dignity. This is the tragic view that Mr. Muir cries up—life as joy triumphing over fate. "For the character of tragedy is not negative and condemnatory, but deeply affirmative and joyous." The ideal man is not the time-serving slave of Christendom, in endless terror of God, forever flattering and bribing God, but the Nietzschean *Ja-sager,* the yes-sayer, facing destiny courageously and a bit proudly, living to the full the life that lies within his grasp in the present, accepting its terms as he finds them, undaunted by the impenetrable shadows that loom ahead.

What Mr. Muir, following Nietzsche, is most dissatisfied with in the modern spirt is its intolerable legalism—its fatuous frenzy to work everything out to nine places of constabulary decimals, to establish windy theories and principles, to break the soul of man to a rule. In part, of course, that effort is of respectable enough origin. It springs from intelligent self-assertion, healthy curiosity, the sense of competence; it is a by-product of the unexampled conquests of nature that have gone on in the modern age. But in other parts it is no more than a by-product of the democratic spirit, the rise of the inferior, the emancipation of the essentially in competent. Science is no longer self-sufficient, isolated from moral ideas, an end in itself; it tends to become a mere agent of mob tyranny; it takes on gratuitous and incomprehensible duties and responsibilities; like the theology that it has supplanted, it has friendlier and friendlier dealings with the secular arm. And art, too, begins to be poisoned by this moral obsession of the awakened proletariat. It ceases to be an expression of well-being, of healthy functioning, of unpolluted joy in life, and becomes a thing of obscure and snuffling purposes, a servant of some low enterprise of the cocksure. The mob is surely no scientist and no artist; it is, in fact, eternally the anti-scientist, the anti-artist; science and art offer it unscalable heights and are hence its enemies. But in a world dominated by mob yearnings and mob passions, even science and art must take on some colour from below. The enemies, if they cannot be met and overthrown on a fair field, can at least be degraded. And when the mob degrades, it always degrades to moral tunes. Morality is its one avenue to superiority— false but none the less soothing. It can always be good. It can always dignify its stupidity, its sordidness and its cowardice with terms borrowed from ethical revelation. The good man is a numskull, but nevertheless he is good.

Mr. Muir has at the modern spirit on many other counts, but nearly all of them may be converted with more or less plausibility into an objection to its ethical obsession, its idiotic craze to legislate and admonish. When he says, for example, that realism in the novel and the drama is hollow, he leaves his case but half stated; there is undoubtedly a void where imagination, feeling and a true sense of the tragic ought to be, but it is filled with the common garbage of mob thinking, to wit, with the common garbage of moral purpose. All of the chief realists, from Zola to Barbusse, are pre-eminently moralists disguised as scientists; what one derives from them, reading them sympathetically, is not illumination but merely indignation. They are always violently against something—and that something is usually the fact that the world is not as secure and placid a place as a Methodist Sunday-school. Their affectation of moral agnosticism need deceive no one. They are secretly appalled (and delighted) by their own "scientific" pornographies, just as their brethren of the vice crusades are appalled and delighted. Realism, of course, can never be absolute. It must always stress something and leave out something. What it commonly stresses is the colossal failure of society to fit into an orderly scheme of causes and effects, virtues and rewards, crimes and punishments. What it leaves out is the glow of romance that hangs about that failure—the poignant drama of blind chance, the fascination of the unknowable. The realists are bad artists because they are anæsthetic to beauty. And a good many scientists are bad scientists for precisely the same reason. In their hands the gorgeous struggle of man against the mysteries and foul ambuscades of nature is converted into a banal cause before a police court, with the complainant put on the stand to prove that his own hands are clean. One cannot read some of the modern medical literature, particularly on the side of public hygiene, without giving one's sympathy to the tubercle bacilli and the spirochætæ. Science of that sort ceases to be a fit concern for men of dignity, superior men, gentlemen; it becomes a concern for evangelists, uplifters, bounders. Its aim is no longer to penetrate the impenetrable, to push forward the bounds of human knowledge, to overreach the sinister trickeries of God; its aim is simply to lengthen the lives of human ciphers and to reinforce their delusion that they confer a favour upon the universe by living at all. Worse, it converts the salvation of such vacuums into a moral obligation, and sets up the absurd doctrine that human progress is furthered by diminishing the death-rate in the Balkans, by rescuing Georgia crackers from the hookworm and by reducing the whole American people, the civilized minority with the barbarian mass, to a race of teetotalling ascetics, full of pious indignations and Freudian suppressions.

The western world reeks with this new sentimentality. It came on in Europe with the fall of feudalism and the rise of the lower orders. Even war, the last surviving enterprise of natural man, has been transformed from a healthy play of innocent instincts into a combat of moral ideas, nine-tenths of them obviously unsound. It no longer offers a career to a Gustavus Adolphus, a Prince Eugene or a Napoleon I. It loses even the spirit of gallant adventure that dignified the theological balderdash of the Crusades—in which, as every one knows, the balderdash was quickly absorbed altogether by the adventure. It becomes the business of specialists in moral indignation. The modern general must not only know the elements of military science; he must also show some of the gifts of a chautauqua orator, including particularly the gift of right-thinking; it would do him more harm to speak of his opponent with professional politeness, as one lawyer might speak of another, than it would do him to lose an important battle. Worse, war gets out of the hands of soldiers altogether. It becomes an undertaking of boob-bumpers, spy-hunters, emotion-pumpers, propaganda-mongers—all sorts of disgusting cads. Its great prizes tend to go, not to the men fighting in the field, but to the man manufacturing shells, alarms, and moral indignation. At the time of the last great series of wars it was said that every musketeer of France carried a marshal's baton in his haversack. The haversack of the musketeer now contains only official literature, informing him of the causes of the war as most lately determined, the names of its appointed moral heroes, and the penalties for discussing its aims, for swapping tobacco with the boys on the other side, and for inviting a pretty peasant-girl into his shell-hole. The baton is being fought for by a press-agent, a labour leader and a Y.M.C.A. secretary.

It is against such degradations that Mr. Muir raises his voice, and in particular against such degradations in the field of the fine arts. The superficial, I daresay, will mistake him (once they get over the sheer immorality of his relation to Nietzsche) as simply one more pleader for *l'art pour l'art*—one more prophet of a superior and disembodied æstheticism. Well, turn to his singularly acute and accurate estimate of Walter Pater: there is the answer to that error. He has, in fact, no leanings whatsoever in any such direction. The thing he argues for, despite all his fury against the debasement of art to mob uses, is not an art that shall be transcendental, but an art that shall relate itself to life primarily and unashamedly, an art that shall accept and celebrate life. He preaches, of course, out of season. There has never been a time in the history of the world when the natural delight of man in himself was held in greater suspicion.

Christianity, after two thousand years, seems triumphant at last. From the ashes of its barbaric theology there arises the phoenix of its maudlin sentimentality; the worship of inferiority becomes its dominating cult. In all directions that worship goes on. It gives a new colour to politics, and not only to politics, but also to the sciences and the arts. Perhaps we are at the mere beginning of the process. The doctrine that all men are equal in the sight of God is now defended and propagated by machine guns; it becomes a felony to deny it; one is already taxed in America to make good the lofty aspirations of Poles, Jugo-Slavs and Armenians. In England there are signs of a further step. An Ehrlich or a Koch, miraculously at work there, might be jailed for slitting the throat of a white rat: all the lower animals, too, it appears, are God's creatures. So viewed, a guinea-pig becomes the peer of a Beethoven, as a farm-hand is already the peer of a Bach. It is too late to turn back; let us hope that the logic of it is quickly worked out to its unescapable conclusion. Once the *pediculus vestimenti* and the streptococcus are protected, there will be a chance again, it may be, for the law of natural selection to achieve its benign purgation.

Meanwhile, Mr. Muir cannot expect his ideas to get much attention. A gaudy parade is passing and the populace is busy cheering. Nevertheless, they were ideas worth playing with, and they are now worth printing and pondering. It seems to me that, in more than one way, they help to illuminate the central æsthetic question—the problem as to the nature and function of artistic representation. They start from Nietzschean beginnings, but they get further than Nietzsche ever got. His whole æsthetic was hampered by the backwardness of psychology in his time. He made many a brilliant guess, but more than once he was hauled up rather sharply by his ignorance of the machinery of thought. Mr. Muir not only has Nietzsche behind him; he also has Freud, as he shows, for example, in §145. Beyond him there is still a lot of room. He will not stop the parade—but he will help the next man.

Edwin Muir was born in the Orkney Islands in 1887. His father was a small crofter there. When he was fourteen years old the family moved to Glasgow. Within four years his father, his mother and two older brothers died, and he was forced to fend for himself. He became a clerk in a Glasgow office and remained there until very recently, when he moved to London. Like all other young men with the itch to write, he tried poetry before prose, and his first verses were printed in *The New Age*. But his discovery of Nietzsche, at the age of twenty-two, exerted such a powerful influence upon him that he soon turned to prose, and five or six years later his first philosophical speculations were printed, again in *The New Age*. They attracted attention and were republished in book-form, in 1918, as "We Moderns." At the last minute the author succumbed to modesty and put the *nom de plume* of Edward Moore upon his book. But now, in this American edition (for which he has made certain revisions), he returns to his own name.

H. L. MENCKEN.

I
THE OLD AGE

1

The Advanced

Among the advanced one observes a strange contradiction: the existence in one and the same person of confidence and enthusiasm about certain aspects of life along with diffidence and pessimism about life itself. The advanced have made up their minds about all the problems of existence but not about the problem of existence. In dealing with these problems they find their greatest happiness; they are there sure-footed, convinced and convincing. But brought face to face with that other problem, how helpless, vacillating and spiritless are they! What! are propaganda, reform, and even revolution, perchance, with many of them simply their escape from their problem?

2

The Intellectual Coquettes

An intellectual coquetry is one of the worst vices of this age. From what does it arise? From fear of a decision? Or from love of freedom? It cannot be from the latter, for to abstain from a choice is not freedom but irresponsibility. To be free, is, on the contrary, itself a choice, a decision involving, in its acceptance, responsibility. And it is responsibility that the intellectual coquettes fear: rather than admit that one burden they will bear all the others of scepticism, pessimism and impotence. To accept a new gospel, to live it out in all its ramifications, is too troublesome, too dangerous. The average man in them pleads, "Be prudent! Where may not this resolution lead you? Through what perils? Into what hells?" And so they remain in their prison house of doubt, neither Pagans nor Christians, neither Theists nor Atheists, ignorant of the fact that they are slaves and that a decision would set them free.

But in the end the soul has its revenge, for their coquetry destroys not only the power but the will to choose. To flirt with dangerous ideas in a graceful manner: that becomes their destiny. For the intellectual coquette, like other coquettes, dislikes above everything passion—passion with its seriousness, sincerity and—demand for a decision.

3

Modern Realism

How crude and shallow is the whole theory of modern realism: a theory of art by the average man for the average man! It makes art intelligible by simplifying or popularizing it; in short, as Nietzsche would say, by vulgarizing it. The average man perceives, for instance, that there is in great drama an element of representation. Come, he says, let us make the representation as "thorough" as possible! Let every detail of the original be reproduced! Let us have life as it is lived! And when he has accomplished this, when representation has become reproduction, he is very well pleased and thinks how far he has advanced beyond the poor Greeks. But it is hardly so! For the Greeks did not aim at the reproduction but at the interpretation of life, for which they would accept no symbol less noble than those *ideal* figures which move in the world of classical tragedy. To the Greeks, indeed, the world of art was precisely this world: not a paltry, sober and conscientious dexterity in the "catching" of the aspects of existence (nothing so easy!), but a symbolizing of the deepest questions and enigmas of life—a thing infinitely more noble, profound and subtle than realistic art. The Greeks would have demanded of realism, Why do you exist? What noble end is served by the reproduction of ordinary existence? Are you not simply superfluous—and vilely smelling at that? And realism could have given no reply, for the truth is that realism *is* superfluous. It is without a *raison d'être*.

The average man, however, takes a second glance at classical tragedy and reaches a second discovery. There is something enigmatical, he finds, behind the Greek clearness of representation, something unexplained; in short, a problem. This problem, however, is not sufficiently clear. Let us state our problems clearly, he cries! Let us have problems which can be recognized at a glance by every one! Let us write a play about "the marriage question," or bad-housing, or the Labour Party! But, again, the theory of the Greeks, at least before Euripides, was altogether different. The "problem" in their tragedies was precisely not a problem which could be stated in a syllogism or solved in a treatise: it was the eternal problem, and it was not stated to be "solved."

Thus the Moderns, in their attempt to simplify art, to understand it or misunderstand it—what does it matter which word is used?—have succeeded in destroying it. The realistic and the "problem" drama alike are for the inartistic. The first is drama without a *raison d'être*, the second is a *raison d'être* without drama.

4

The Modern Tragic

In realistic novels and dramas a new type of the tragic has been evolved. It may be called tragedy without a meaning. In classical and Shakespearean tragedy, the inevitable calamities incident to human existence were given significance and nobility by the poets. That interpretive power of drama was, indeed, the essential thing to the great artists, to whom representation was only a means. But the realists with their shallow rationalizing of art have changed all that. They have cut out the essential part of drama so as to make the other part more "complete": in short, their tragedy is now simply "tragedy" in the newspaper sense. And it is obvious that this kind of "art" is much easier to produce than tragedy in the grand style: one has not even to read a meaning into it. This absence of meaning, however, is itself, in the long run, made to appear the last word of an unfathomably ironical wisdom. And in this light, how much modern wisdom is understood! The superficiality which can see only the surface here parades as the profundity which has dived into every abyss and found it empty. No! it is not tragedy but the modern tragedian who is without a *raison d'être!*

5

Realism as a Symptom of Poverty

In an age in which the power of creation is weak, men will choose the easiest forms: those in which sustained elevation is not demanded and creation itself is eked out in various ways. The world of our day has therefore as its characteristic production the realistic novel, which in form is more loose, in content and execution more unequal, and in imaginative power less rich and inventive than poetic drama, or *any* of the higher forms of literature. If we deduct from the modern "literary artist," the diarist, the sociologist, the reporter, and the collector of documents, there is not much left. For creation there is very little room in his works; perhaps it is as well!

6

Compliments and Art

The convention of gallantry observed by the sexes is the foundation of all refined understanding between them. For in the mutual game of compliment it is the spiritual attitude and not the spoken word that matters. There is truth in this attitude, however unreal the words may seem: a thousand times more truth than in the modern egalitarian, go-as-you-please camaraderie of the sexes. Here there is truth neither in the spirit nor in the letter. To be candid, about this new convention there is something faintly fatuous: the people who act thus are not subtle! Yet they are hardly to be blamed; it is the age that is at fault. There is no time for reflection upon men, women and manners, and consequently no refinement of understanding, no form in the true sense. We work so hard and have so little leisure that when we meet we are tired and wish to "stretch our legs," as Nietzsche said. It is far from our thoughts that a convention between men and women might be *necessary*; we are not disposed to inquire why this convention arose; it presents itself to us as something naively false; and we have time only to be unconventional.

The ceremonious in manners arose from the recognition that between the sexes there must be distance—respect as well as intimacy—understanding. The old gallantry enabled men and women to be intimate and distant at the same time: it was the perfection of the art of manners. Indeed, we can hardly have sufficient respect for this triumphant circumvention of a natural difficulty, whereby it was made a source of actual pleasure. But now distance and understanding have alike disappeared. The moderns, so obtuse have they become, see here no difficulty at all, consequently no need for manners: brotherhood—comradeship—laziness has superseded that. Nothing is any longer *understood;* but a convention means essentially that something is understood. Indeed, it is already a gaucherie to explain the meaning of a good convention. But what can one do? Against obtuseness the only weapon is obtuseness.

In literature this decline into bad taste and denseness is most clearly to be seen. So incapable have readers become, so resourceless writers, that whatever is said now must be said right out; sex must be called sex; and no one has sufficient subtlety to suggest or to follow a suggestion. Hence, Realism. An artist has to write exactly what he means: the word must be word and nothing more. But this is to misunderstand art. For the words of the true artist undergo a transubstantiation and become flesh and blood, even spirit. His words are deeds—to say nothing of what he writes *between* his lines! Realism in art and "comradeship" between the sexes are two misunderstandings, or, rather, two aspects of a misunderstanding. And that misunderstanding is perhaps attributable to a lack of leisure? And that to modern hurry? And that to the industrial system?

7

A Modern Problem

It has been observed again and again that as societies—forms of production, of government, and so on—become more complex, the mastery of the individual over his destiny grows weaker. In other words, the more man subjugates "nature," the more of a slave he becomes. The industrial system, for instance, which is the greatest modern example of man's subjugation of nature, is at the same time the greatest modern example of man's enslavement. What are we to think, then? Is the problem a moral one, and shall we say that a conquest of nature which is not preceded by a conquest of human nature is bound to be bad? In a society which has not surpassed the phase of slavery does every addition to man's power over nature simply intensify the slavery? Or is the problem intellectual? And when the intellect concentrates upon one branch of knowledge to the neglect of the other, is the outcome bound to be the enslavement of the others? For instance the nineteenth century devoted far more of its brains to industry than to politics—its politics, indeed, was merely the reflection of its industry—with the result that industry has now enslaved us all. Yes, it has enslaved us all—not merely the wage-earners, not merely the salariat! In the old days the workman, indeed, was a slave, but now the employer is a slave as well.

In this age, therefore, in which man appears as the helpless appendage of a machine too mighty for him, it is natural that theories of Determinism should flourish. It is natural, also, that the will should become weak and discouraged, and, consequently, that the power of creation should languish. And so the world of art has withered and turned barren. The artist needs above all things a sense of power; it is out of the abundance of this sense that he creates. But confronted with modern society, that vast machine, and surrounded by its hopeless mechanics and slaves, he feels the sense dying within him; nor does the evil cease there, for along with the sense of power, power itself dies.

Well, does not the moral become clearer and clearer? If art and literature are to flourish again, artists, writers, nay, the whole community must regain the sense of power. Therefore, economic emancipation first!

8

Leisure and Good Things

The very greatest danger confronts a people who renounce leisure: that people will become shallow—just consider England! For of all things noble it is hard to see the immediate utility: patience and reverence are needed before one can see in them a meaning at all. Art, literature and philosophy are not obvious goods: at the first glance they appear even repellent: alas, then, for them in an age of first glances! In such an age, it is true, they will not altogether disappear. Something worse will happen. They will be degraded, made obvious, misunderstood; in one word, popularized—the fate of our time. Society should be organized so as to give to its members the maximum of leisure; thus would the dissemination of art and philosophy be made at least possible. But society should at the same time provide for a privileged class of artists and philosophers, with *absolute* leisure, who would work only when the inner compulsion made them. The second condition is at least as important as the first.

9

Wanted: A History of Hurry

Is there a critic who wishes to be at once edifying and entertaining? Let him write a history of hurry in its relation to literature and art. Has literature decayed as hurry has intensified? Have standards of balance, repose and leisured grace gradually shrunk since, say, the Industrial Revolution? Has the curtailment of the realm of literature, its reduction from the Romantic school to the Victorian circle and from that to the Decadent clique, been due to the everstrengthening encroachment of hurry? And has hurry now become finally triumphant so that our critics and even our artists and savants are nothing more than journalists? For certainly they seem to be so.

These are questions to be investigated by our historian.

10

The Sex Novel

How did the vogue of the sex novel arise? Perhaps from the great attention which was in the last century given to the sciences of biology and physiology; and perhaps, more especially from the popularization of these sciences. Love was, under the spell of science, translated by the novelists into sex. Not the psychology, but the physiology of love was found interesting: with the result that for the production of a modern novel one qualification alone is now necessary: a "knowledge of the simple facts of physiology," as the primer-writers say. Well, what is the remedy for this? Not a denial of physiology: those who have learned it cannot now erase it from their memory and become voluntarily ignorant. No; let, rather, the opposite course be taken! Let us popularize psychology as well!

11

These Advanced People

A. Free Love is all right in theory, but all wrong in practice. B. On the contrary! I think it is all right in practice, but all wrong in theory.

12

Sex in Literature

In English literature, until very modern times, sex was treated only within the limits of a very well-understood convention. From this convention the physiological was strictly excluded. Yet, of our classical writers, even in the most artificial periods, it cannot be said that they did not understand sex. No matter how "unreal" they might be in writing about Love, the physiological contingencies of Love were unmistakably implied in their works, but only, it is true, implied. The moderns, however, saw in this treatment of Love nothing but a convention, a "lie"; and they became impatient of the artificiality, as if art could be anything but artificial! To what was the change of attitude due? Not to a failure in the artistic convention: that was perfectly sound. No, it was the reader who had failed: a generation of readers had arisen who had not learnt the art of reading, who did not understand reading as a cultured amateur of the eighteenth century, for instance, understood it. Literature was to this reader a document, not an art. He had no eye for what is written between the lines—for symbolism, idealization, "literature." And it was to satisfy him that the realistic school arose: it arose, indeed, out of himself. In the realist the modern reader has become writer: the man who could not learn the art of reading has here essayed the more difficult art of writing—documentary art!

13

History of a Realist

Who will write a series of biographies of modern writers, illustrating this thesis: that they are nothing more than modern readers wielding a hasty pen? Such a set of memoirs would almost compensate us for having read the works of these writers. How interesting, for instance, it would be to know how many years—surely it would be years?—they spent in trying to understand literature before they dedicated themselves to its service. How interesting, again, to discover how many hours each day X, the celebrated novelist, devotes to contemplation, how many to writing for the newspapers, and how many to his present masterpiece. What!

one hour's thought has actually preceded five hours' dictation! This revelation is, after all, not so startling. On second thought, these memoirs seem superfluous; we can read everything we wish to know of the moderns in their works.

Yet, for our better amusement, will not some one write his one and only novel, giving the true history of the novelist? A novel against novels! But for that we need a second Cervantes, yet how unlike the first! For on this occasion it is not Don Quixote that must be satirized, but Sancho Panza.

14

Novelists by Habit

All of us who read are novelists more or less nowadays: that is to say, we collect "impressions," "analyse" ourselves, make a pother about sex, and think that people, once they are divorced, live happily ever after. The habit of reading novels has turned us into this! When one of us becomes articulate, however—in the form of a novel—he only makes explicit his kinship with the rest; he proclaims to all the world that he is a mediocrity.

15

The Only Course

All the figures in this novel are paltry; we despise them, and, if we were in danger of meeting them in real life, would take steps to avoid them; yet such is the author's adroitness that we are led on helplessly through the narrative, through unspeakable sordidness of circumstance and soul, hating ourselves and him, and feeling nothing better than slaves. To rouse our anxiety lest Herbert lose five pounds, or Mabel find it impossible to get a new dress, this is art, this is modern art! But to feel *anxiety* about such things is ignoble; and to live in a sordid atmosphere, even if it be of a book, is the part of a slave. And yet we cannot but admire. For in this novel what subtlety in the treatment there must be overlying the fundamental vulgarity of the theme! How is Art, which should make Man free, here transformed into a potent means for enslaving him! It is impossible to yield oneself to the sway of a modern realist without a loss in one's self-respect. To what is due this conspicuous absence of nobility in modern writers? But is the question, indeed, worth the asking? For to the artist and to him who would retain freedom of soul, there is only one course with the paltry in literature—to avoid it.

16

The Average Man

It is surely one of G. K. Chesterton's paradoxes that he praises the average man. For he is not himself an average man, but a man of genius; he does not write of the average man, but of grotesques; he is not read by the average man, but by intellectuals and the nonconformist middle-class. The true prophets of the average man are the popular realistic novelists. For they write of him and for him—yes, even when they write "for themselves," when they are "serious artists." Who, then, but them should extol him? It is their *métier*.

17

The "New" Writers

The fault of the most modern writers—and especially of the novelists—is not that they are too modern, but that they are too traditional. It is true, they are not traditional in the historical manner of G. K. Chesterton, who wishes to destroy one tradition—the modern tradition—in order to get back to another—the mediæval. To Mr. Chesterton tradition is a matter of selection; the dead tradition seems to him nobler than the living; and, deliberately, therefore, he would return to it. The new writers, however, follow a tradition also, though a much narrower one; they, too, believe in the past, but only, alas, in the immediate past; they are slaves to the generation which preceded theirs. In short, that which is disgusting in them is their inability to rise high enough to *see* their little decade or two, and to challenge it, if they cannot from the standpoint of a nobler future, then, at least, from that of the noblest past. But how weak must a generation be which is not strong enough to challenge and supersede Arnold Bennett, for instance.

18

The Modern Reader

What is it that the modern reader demands from those who write for him? To be challenged, and again to be challenged, and evermore to be challenged—but on no account to be asked to accept a challenge, on no account to be expected to take sides! A seat at the tournament is all that he asks, where he may watch the most sincere and intrepid spirits of his time waging their desperate battle and spilling their life blood upon the sand. How he loves them when, with high gesture, they fling down their gauntlets and utter their blasphemies! His heart then exults within him; but, why? Simply because he is a connoisseur; simply because he *collects*gauntlets!

19

The Public

Of the modern writers who are in earnest, Mr. Chesterton has had the most ironical fate: he has been read by the people who will never agree with him. To the average man for whom he writes he is an intellectual made doubly inaccessible by his orthodoxy and his paradox. It is the advanced, his *bête noire,*who read him, admire him, and—disagree with him.

20

Reader and Writer

The modern reader loves to be challenged. The modern writer, if he is in earnest, however, is bound to challenge him. This is his greatest burden; that he *must* fall a victim of the advanced idlers. But one day he thinks he sees a way of escape. He has noticed that the reader desires not only to be challenged, but to be able to understand the challenge at a glance. And here he sees his advantage. I shall write, he says, to himself, in a manner beautiful, exact, and yet not easily understood; so I shall throw off the intellectual coquettes and secure my audience of artists, for my style is beautiful; an audience of critics, for my style is exact; an audience of patient, resolute, conscientious intellects, for my style is difficult. This, perhaps, was the conscious practice of Nietzsche. But he did not foresee that, for the benefit of the intellectual coquettes, who must have hold of new thoughts by one end or another, a host of popularizers would be born; he did not reckon with the Nietzscheans!

21

Popularity

How amazingly popular he is. Even the man in the street reads him. Yes; but it is because he has first read the man in the street.

22

Middle Age's Betrayals

It is not easy to tell by a glance what is the character of a young man; his soul has not yet etched itself clearly enough upon his body. But one may read a middle-aged man's soul with perfect ease; and not only his soul but his history. For when a man has passed five-and-forty, he looks—not what he is, perhaps—but certainly what he has been. If he has been invariably respectable, he is now the very picture of respectability. If he has been a man about town or a secret toper, the fact is blazoned so clearly on his face that even a child can read it. If he has studied, his very walk, to use a phrase of Nietzsche's, is learned. As for the poet, we know how terribly poetical he looks in middle age—poor devil! Well, to every one of you, I say, Beware!

23

The Novelists and the Artist

Is it the modern novelists who are to be blamed for the degraded image of the artist which lives in the minds of the cultured populace? Turgenieff in "On the Eve," and Henry James in "Roderick Hudson" display the artist simply as a picturesque waster, an oh so charming, impulsive, childlike, naïve waster. But, in doing so, they surely confused the artist with the man of artistic temperament. Of the artistic temperament, however, the great artists had very often little or nothing—far less, certainly, than either Shubin or Roderick. The great examples of last century, the Goethes, Ibsens, and Nietzsches, knew that there were qualities more essential to them than temperament; discipline, for instance, perseverance, truth to themselves, self-control. How is it possible, indeed, without these virtues—virtues of the most difficult and heroic kind—for the artist to bring his gifts to maturity, to become great? His discipline to beauty must be as severe as the discipline of the saint to holiness. And, then, how has his sensuousness been misconstrued and vulgarized; and treated precisely, indeed, as if it were the licentiousness of a present-day Tom Jones! That artists can be thought about in such a way proves only one thing, namely, in what poor esteem they are now held. We need a new ideal of the artist; or, failing that, an old one, that of Plato, perhaps, or of Leonardo, or of Nietzsche.

24

Decadence and Health

It is in the decadent periods that the most triumphantly healthy men—one or two—appear. The corrupt Italy of the Renaissance gave birth to Leonardo; the Europe of Gautier, Baudelaire and Wilde produced Nietzsche. In decadent eras both disease and health become more self-conscious; they are cultivated, enhanced and refined. It has been said that the best way to remain healthy is not to think of health. But lack of self-consciousness speaks here. Perhaps the Middle Ages were as diseased as our own—only they did not know it! Is decadence nothing more than the symptom of a self-conscious age? And is "objectivity" the antidote? Well, we might believe this if we could renounce our faith that mankind will yet become healthy—if we could become optimists in the present-day sense!

25

Art in Modern Society

An object of beauty has in modern surroundings a dangerous seduction which it did not possess in less hideous eras. In this is there to be found a contributory explanation of Decadence—the decadent being one who feels the power of beauty intensely, and the repulsion from his environment as intensely, and who plunges into the enjoyment of beauty madly, with abandonment? In a society, however, which was not hideous as ours is, and in which beauty was distributed widely over all the aspects and forms of existence, the intoxication of beauty would not be felt with the same terrible intensity; a beautiful object would be enjoyed simply as one among many lovely things. In short, it would be enjoyed in the manner of health, not in that of sickness. It is the *contrast* that is dangerous; the aridity of modern life arouses a terrible thirst, which is suddenly presented with the spectacle of a beauty unaccountable and awful; and this produces a dislocation and convulsion of the very soul. So that the present-day artist, if he would retain his health—if he would remain an artist—must curb his very love of the beautiful, and treat beauty, when he meets it, as he always does, in the gutter, a little cynically. Otherwise he will lose his wits, and Art will become his Circe. Therefore, mockery and hard laughter—alas, that it *must* be so!

26

Art in Industry

In those wildernesses of dirt, ugliness and obscenity, our industrial towns, there are usually art galleries, where the daintiest and most beautiful things, the flowers of Greek statuary, for instance, bloom among the grime like a band of gods imprisoned in a slum. The spectacle of art in such surroundings sometimes strikes us as being at once ludicrous and pathetic, like something delicate and lovely sprawling in the gutter, or an angel with a dirty face.

27

Conventions

The revolt against conventions in art, thought, life and manners may be due to at least more than one cause. It is usually ascribed to "vitality" which "breaks through" forms, because it desires to be "free." But common sense tells us that more than two or three of our friends abjure convention for an altogether different reason—to be candid, on account of a *lack* of vitality resulting in laziness and the inability to endure restraint of any kind. And, for the others, we shall judge their "vitality" to be justified when they build new conventions worthy of observance, instead of running their heads finally into illimitable space. Or does their strength not go just so far? There is something suspicious about this vitality which cannot create: it resembles impotence so much! Heaven preserve the moderns from their "vitality"!

28

"Vitality"

When moderns talk of the "vitality" of their most lauded writer, what they mean is finally the size of his muscles, physical energy, or, at the most, strong emotions; not vigour of mind. Well, let us on no account make the opposite mistake and revile the large muscle and energetic feelings: they are admirable things. Let us point out, however, that vitality of emotion undisciplined by vitality of thought leads nowhere, is often disruptive and cannot build. But to build is our highest duty and our peculiar form of freedom—we who have realized that there is no freedom without power. As for the old freedom—it is only the slaves who are not already tired of it.

Decadence

The decisive thing, determining whether an artist shall be major or minor, is very often not artistic at all, but moral. Yes, though it shock our modern ears, let this be proclaimed! The more "temperament" an artist has, the more character he requires to govern it, to make it fruitful for him, if he would not have it get beyond control, and wreck both him and itself. And, consequently, the great artists show, as a rule, less "temperament" than the minor; they appear more self-contained and less "artistic." Indeed, they smile with the hint of irony at the merely "artistic."

It is, perhaps, when the traditions of artistic morality and discipline have broken down, when the "temperament" has, therefore, become unfettered and lawless, that decadence in art is born. The sincerity of the artist, his chief virtue, is gone—the sincerity which commands him to create only under the pressure of an artistic necessity, which tells him, in other words, to produce nothing which is not genuine. Without sincerity, severity and patience, nothing great in art can be created. And it is precisely in these virtues that the decadent is lacking. A love of beauty is his only credential as an artist, but, undisciplined, it degenerates very soon into a love of mere effect. An effect of beauty at all costs, whether it be the true beauty or not! That becomes his object. Without a root in any soil, he aspires to the condition of the water lily, and, in due time, becomes a full-blown æsthete. Is it because he is incapable of becoming anything else? Has he in despair grown "artistic" simply because he is not an artist? Is Decadence the most subtle disguise of impotence? And are decadents those who, if they had submitted to an artistic discipline of sincerity, would never have written at all? Of some of them this is true, but of others it is not; and in that lies the tragedy of Decadence. Wilde himself was, perhaps, a decadent by misadventure; for on occasion he could rise above decadence into sincerity. "The Ballad of Reading Gaol" proves that. He was the victim of a bad æsthetic morality, to which, it is true, he had a predisposition. And if this is true of him, it is true, also, of his followers. A baleful artistic ethic still rules, demoralizing the young artist at the moment when he should be disciplining himself; and turning, perhaps, some one with the potentiality of greatness into a minor artist. By neglecting the harder virtues, the decadents have made minor art inevitable and great art almost impossible.

The old tradition of artistic discipline must be regained, then, or a new and even more severe tradition inaugurated. A text-book of morality for artists is now overdue. When it has been written, and the new discipline has been hailed and submitted to by the artists, who can say if greatness may not again be possible?

Decadence Again

How is the dissolution of the tradition of artistic discipline to be explained? To what cause is it to be traced? Perhaps to the more general dissolution of tradition which has taken place in modern times. When theological dogmas and moral values are thrown into the melting-pot, and the discipline of centuries is dissolved into anarchy, it is natural that artistic traditions should perish along with them. Decadence follows free-thought: it appears at the time when the old values lie deliquescent and the new values have not yet risen, the dry land has not yet appeared. But this does not happen always: the old traditions of morality, theology, politics and industry are overthrown, the beginnings of a new tradition appear tentatively, everything fixed has vanished, the wildest hopes and the most chilling despair are the common possession of one and the same generation—but, throughout, the artistic tradition is held securely and confidently, it remains the one thing fixed in a world of dissolution. Then an art arises greater even than that of the eras of tradition. The pathos of the dying and the inexpressible hope of the newly born find expression side by side; all chains are broken, and the world appears suddenly to be immeasurable. Is this what happened at the Renaissance?

31

Wilde

The refined degeneracy of Oscar Wilde might be explained on the assumption that he was at once over—and under—civilized: he had acquired all the exquisite and superfluous without the necessary virtues. These "exquisite" virtues are unfortunately dangerous to all but those who have become masters of the essential ones; they are qualities of the body more than of the mind; they are developments and embellishments of the shell of man. In acquiring them, Wilde ministered to his body merely, and, as a consequence, it became more and more powerful and subtle—far more powerful and subtle than his mind. Eventually this body—senses, passions and appetite—actually became the intellectual principle in him, of which his mind was merely a drugged and stupefied slave!

32

Wilde and the Sensualists

The so-called Paganism of our time, the movement towards sensualism of the followers of Wilde, is not an attempt, however absurd, to supersede Christianity; nor is it even in essence anti-Christian. At the most it is a reaction—not a step beyond current religion into a new world of the spirit, but a changing from one foot to the other, a reliance on the senses for a little, so that the over-laboured soul may rest. And there is still much of Christianity in this modern Paganism. Its devotees are too deeply corrupted to be capable either of pure sensuousness or of pure spirituality. They speak of Christ like voluptuaries, and of Eros like penitents. But it is impossible now to become a Pagan: one must remember Ibsen's Julian and take warning. Two thousand years of "bad conscience," of Christian self-probing, with its deepening of the soul, cannot be disavowed, forgotten, unlived. For Paganism a simpler spirit, mind and sensuousness are required than we can reproduce. We cannot feel, we cannot think, above all, we cannot feel without thinking of our feelings, as the Pagans did. Our modern desire to take out our soul and look at it separates us from the naïve classic sensuousness.

What, then, does modern sensualism mean? What satisfaction does it bring to those, by no means few in number, its "followers"? A respite, an escapade, a holiday from Christianity, from the inevitable. For Christianity is assumed by them to be the inevitable, and it fills them with the loathing which is evoked by the enforced contemplation of things tyrannical and permanent. To escape from it they plunge madly into sensuality as into a sea of redemption. But the disgust which drives them there will eventually drive them forth again—into asceticism and the denial of the senses. Christianity will then appear stronger than ever, having been purged of its "uncleanness." Yes, the sensualists of our time are the best unconscious friends of Christianity, its "saviours," who have taken its sins upon their shoulders.

There still remain the few who do not assume Christianity to be inevitable, who desire, no matter how hopeless the fight may seem, to surmount it, and who see that men have played too long the game of reaction. "To cure the senses by the soul and the soul by the senses" seems to them a creed for invalids. And, therefore, that against which, above all, they guard, is a mere relapse into sensualism. Not by fleeing from Christianity do they hope to reach their goal; but by understanding it, perhaps by "seeing through" it, certainly by benefiting in so far as they can by it, and, finally, emancipating themselves from it. They know that the soil no longer exists out of which grew the flower of Paganism, and that they must pass through Christianity if they would reach a new sensuality and a new spirituality. But their motto is, Spirituality first, and, after that, only as much sensuality as our spirituality can govern! They hold that as men become more spiritual they may safely become more sensual; but that, to the man without spirit, sensuality and asceticism are alike an indulgence and a curse. That the spirit should rule—such is their desire; but it must rule as a constitutional governor, not as an arbitrary tyrant. For the senses, too, as Heine said, have their rights.

33

Arnold Going Down the Hill

One section of the realist school—that represented by Bennett and John Galsworthy—may be described as a reaction from asceticism. Men had become tired of experiencing Life only in its selected and costly "sensations," and sought an escape from "sensations," sought the ordinary. But another section of the school—George Moore, for example—was merely a bad translation of æstheticism. Equally tired of the exquisite, already having sampled all that luxury in "sensation" could provide, the artists now sought *new "sensations"*—and nothing else—in the squalid. It was the *rôle* of the æsthetes to go downhill gracefully, but when they turned realists they ceased even to do that. They went downhill *sans* art. Yet, in doing so, did they not rob æstheticism of its seductiveness? And should we not, therefore, feel grateful to them? Alas, no; for to the taste of this age, grace and art have little fascination: it is the heavy, unlovely and sordid that seduces. To disfigure æstheticism was to popularize it. And now the very man in the street is—artistically speaking—corrupted: a calamity second in importance only to the corruption of the artists and thinkers.

34

Pater and the Æsthetes

How much of Walter Pater's exclusiveness and reclusiveness was a revulsion from the ugliness of his time—an ugliness which he was not strong enough to contemplate, far less to fight—it is hard to say. Perhaps his phase of the Decadence may be defined as largely a reaction against industrialism, just as that of Wilde may be defined as largely a reaction against Christianity: but, in the former case as in the latter, that against which the reaction was made was assumed to be permanent. Indeed, by escaping from industrialism instead of fighting it, Pater and his followers made its persistence only a little more secure. It is true, there are excuses enough to palliate their weakness: the delicateness of their own nerves and senses, making them peculiarly liable to suffering, the ugliness and apparent invulnerability of industrialism, the beauty and repose of the world of art wherein they might take refuge and be happy. Art as forgetfulness, art as Lethe, the seduction of that cry was strong! But to yield to it was none the less unforgivable: it was an act traitorous not only to society but to art itself. For what was the confession underlying it? That the society of today and of tomorrow is, and *must be*, barren; that no great art can hereafter be produced; that there is nothing left but to enjoy what has been accomplished! Against that presumption, not the Philistines but the great artists will cry as the last word of Nihilism.

Pater's creed marks, therefore, a degradation of the conception of art. Art as something exclusive, fragile and a little odd, the occupation of a few æsthetic eccentrics—this is the most pitiable caricature! To make themselves understood by one another, this little clique invented a jargon of their own; in this jargon Pater's books are written, and not only his, but those of his followers to this day. It is a style lacking, above all, in good taste; it very easily drops into absurdity; indeed, it is always on the verge of absurdity. It has no masculinity, no hardness; and it is meant to be read by people a little insincerely "æsthetic," who are conscious that they are open to ridicule, and who are accordingly indulgent to the ridiculous; the Fabians of art. To admire Pater's style, it is necessary first to put oneself into the proper attitude.

35

Creator and Æsthete

The true creators and the mere æsthetes agree in this, that they are not realists. Neither of them copies existence in its external details: wherein do they differ? In that the creators write of certain realities behind life, and the æsthetes—of the words standing for these realities.

36

Hypocrisy of Words

The æsthetes, and Pater and Wilde in particular, made a cult of the use of decorative words. They demanded, not that a word should be *true*, nor even that it should be true and pretty at the same time, but simply that it should be pretty. It cannot be denied that writers here and there before them had been guilty of using a fine word where a common one was most honest; but this had been generally regarded as a forgiveable, "artistic" weakness. Wilde and his followers, however, chose "exquisite" words systematically, in conformity to an artistic dogma, and held that literature consisted in doing nothing else. And that was dangerous; for truth was thereby banished from the realm of diction and a hypocrisy of words arose. In short, language no longer grasped at realities, and literature ceased to express any thing at all, except a writer's taste in words.

37

The Average Man

In this welter of dissolving values, the intellectuals of our time find themselves struggling, and liable at any moment to be engulfed. A few of them, however, have snatched at something which, in the prevailing deliquescence, appears to be solid—the average man. Encamped upon him, they have won back sanity and happiness. But their act is nevertheless simply a reaction; here the real problem has not yet been faced! What is it that makes the average man more sane and happy than the modern man? The possession of dogmas, says G. K. Chesterton; let us therefore have dogmas! But, alas, for them he goes back and not forward. And not only back, but back to the very dogmas against which modern thought, and Decadence with it, are a reaction, nay, the *inevitable* reaction. What! has Mr. Chesterton, then, postponed the solution of the problem? And on the heels of his remedy does there tread the old disease over again? Perhaps it is so. The acceptance of the old dogmas will be followed by a new reaction from them, a new disintegration of values therefore, and a new Decadence. The hands of the clock can be put back, it is true; but they will eventually reach the time when the hour shall strike *again* for the solution of the modern problem.

And that is the criticism which modern men must pass upon Mr. Chesterton; that he interposed in the course of their malady to bring relief with a remedy which was not a remedy. The modern problem should have been worked out to a new solution, to its own solution. Instead of going back to the old dogmas, we should have strained on towards the new. And if, in this generation, the new dogmas are still out of sight, if we have meantime to live our lives without peace or stability, does it matter so very much? To do so is, perhaps, our allotted task. And as sacrifices to the future we justify our very fruitlessness, our very modernity!

II

ORIGINAL SIN

38

Original Sin

Original Sin and the Future are essentially irreconcilable conceptions. The believer in the future looks upon humanity as plastic: the good and the bad in man are not fixed quantities, always, in every age, past and future, to be found in the same proportions: an "elevation of the type man" is, therefore, possible. But the believer in Original Sin regards mankind as that in which—the less said about the good, the better—there is, at any rate, a fixed substratum of the bad. And *that* can never be lessened, never weakened, never conquered. Therefore, man has to fight constantly to escape the menace of an ever-present defeat. A battle in which victory is impossible; a contest in which man has to climb continually in order not to fall lower; existence as the tread mill: that is what is meant by Original Sin.

And as such it is the great enemy of the Future, the believers in which hold that there is not this metaphysical drag. But it is more. At all things aspiring it sets the tongue in the cheek, gladly provides a caricature for them, and becomes their Sancho Panza. To the great man it says, through the mouths of its chosen apostles, the average men, "What matter how high you climb! This load which you carry even as we will bring you back to us at last. And the higher you climb the greater will be your fall. Humanity cannot rise above its own level." And therefore, humility, equality, radicalism, comradeship in sin—the ideas of Christianity!

39

Again

Distrust of the future springs from the same root as distrust of great men. It derives from the belief in the average man, which derives from the belief in Original Sin. The egalitarian sentiment strives always to become unconditional. It claims not only that all men are equal, but that the men who live now are no more than the equals of those who lived one, or five, thousand years ago, and no less than the equals of those who will live in another one, or five, thousand years. And it desires that this should be so: its jealousy embraces not only the living, but the dead and the unborn.

40

Again

Society is a conspiracy, said Emerson, against the great man. And to blast him utterly in the centre of his being, it invented Original Sin. Is Original Sin, then, a theological dogma or a political device?

41

Equality

Is equality, in truth, a generous dogma? Does it express, as every one assumes, the solidarity of men in their higher attributes? It is time to question this, and to ask if inequality be not the more noble and generous belief. For, surely, it is in their nobler qualities that men are most unequal. It was not in his genius that Shakespeare was only the equal, for instance, of his commentators; it was in the groundwork of his nature, in those feelings and desires without which he would not have been a man at all, in the things which made him human, but which did not make him Shakespeare: in a word, in that which is for us of no significance. Equality in the common part of man's nature, equality in sin, equality before God—it is the same thing—that is the only equality which can be admitted. And if its admission is insisted upon by apologists for Christianity, that is because to the common part of man's nature they give so much importance, because they are believers in Original Sin. In their equality there is accordingly more malice than generosity. The belief that no one is other than themselves, the will that no one shall be other than themselves—there is nothing generous in that belief and that will. For man, according to them, is guilty from the womb. And what, then, is equality but the infinitely consoling consciousness of tainted creatures that every one on this earth is tainted?

The believer in Original Sin will, of course, deny this, and say that in his philosophy men are equals also in their higher *rôle* as "sons of God." But is this so? Is salvation, like sin, common to all men? Is it not, on the contrary, something *conferred* as the reward of a belief and a choice—a belief and a choice which an Atheist, for instance, simply cannot embrace? So that here, touching the highest part of men, their soul, there is introduced, by Christianity itself, a distinction, an inequality—the distinction, the inequality between the "saved" and the "lost." Men are equal inasmuch as they are all damned, but they are not equal inasmuch as they are not all redeemed.

Gazing at man, however, no longer through the eyes of the serpent, shall we not be bound to find, if we look *high* enough, distinction, superiority, inferiority, valuation? The dogma of equality is itself a device to evade valuation. For valuation is difficult, and demands generosity for its exercise. To recognize that one is greater than you, and cheerfully to acknowledge it; to see that another is less than you, and to treat the inferiority as a trifling thing, that is difficult, that requires generosity. But one who believes in inequality will always be looking for greatness in others; his eye, habituated to the contemplation of lofty things, will become subtle in the detection of concealed nobility; while to the ignoble he will give only a glance—and is it not good, where one may not help, to pass on the other side? The egalitarians will cry that it is ungenerous to believe that some men are vile; but it is a strange generosity which would persuade us with them that all men are vile. Let us be frank. To those who believe in the future, inequality is a holy thing; their pledge that greatness shall not disappear from the earth; the rainbow assuring them that Man shall not go down beneath the vast tide of mankind. All great men are to them at once forerunners and sacrifices; the imperfect forms which the Future has shattered in trying to incarnate itself; the sublime ruins of *future* greatness.

42

If Men Were Equal

If men had been equal at the beginning, they would never have risen above the savage. For in absolute equality even the concept of greatness could not have come into being. Inequality is the source of all advancement.

43

The Fall of Man

In very early times men must have had a deep sense of the tragicality of existence: life was then so full of pain; death, as a rule, so sudden and unforeseen, and the world generally so beset with terrors. The few who were fortunate enough to escape violent death had yet to toil incessantly to retain a footing on this unkind star. Life would, accordingly, appear to them in the most sombre tones and colours. And it was to explain this human misfortune, and not sin at all, that the whole fable of Adam and Eve and the Fall was invented. The doctrine of Original Sin was simply an interpretation which was afterwards read into the story, an interpretation, perhaps, as arbitrary as the orthodox interpretation of the Song of Songs.

How would the fable arise? Well, a primitive poet one day in a fit of melancholy made the whole thing up. Out of his misery his desires created for him an imaginary state, its opposite, the Garden of Eden. But this state being created, the problem arose, How did Man fall from it? And the Tree was brought in. But to the naïve, untheological poet, this tree had nothing to do with metaphysics or with sin, the child of metaphysics. It was simply a magical tree, and if Man ate of the fruit of it, something terrible would happen to him. The Fall of Man was a *mystery* to the poet, which he did not rationalize or theologize. Well, Man succumbed to curiosity, and pain and misfortune befell the human race. But we must not assume in the modern manner that with the eating of the fruit early man associated any idea of guilt. Rather the contrary; he regarded the act simply as unfortunate, just as at the present day we regard as unfortunate the foolish princess in some fairy tale. So the Fall was not to him a crime, branding all mankind with a metaphysical stigma.

That conception came much later, when the conscience had become deeper, more subtle and more neurotic; when individualism had been introduced into morality. And at that time, too, the ideal of the Redeemer became vitiated. Early man, if he did envisage a Redeemer, envisaged him as one who would set him back in the Garden of Eden again, in the literal, terrestrial Garden of Eden, be it understood: theology had not yet been etherealized. And this Redeemer would redeem *all* men: the distinction of the individual came afterwards. It was not until later, too, that this ideal was "interpreted," and, as a concession to the conscience, salvation was made a conditional thing: the reward of those who were successful in a competition in credulity, in which the first prize went to the most simple, most stupid. The "guilt" now implicated in the Fall was not purged away from all men by the Redeemer, but only from such as would "accept" it. And, lastly, with the passing of Jesus, the redemption was still further de-actualized. It was found that acceptance of the Redeemer did *not* reinstate Man in an earthly Garden: paradise was, therefore, drawn on the invisible wires of theology into the inaccessible heavens. Salvation lay at the other side of the grave, and there it was safe from assault.

Nevertheless, what our primitive poet meant by the Fall and the Redemption was probably something entirely different. The Fall to him was the fall into misfortune, not into sin: the Redemption to him was the redemption from misfortune, not from sin. And his Redeemer would be, therefore—whom? Perhaps it is impossible for us to imagine the nature of such a being.

This is not an interpretation, but an attempted explanation of the story of the Fall.

44

Interpretations

How inexhaustible is myth! In the story of the Fall is a meaning for every age and every creed. The interpretation called Original Sin is only one of a thousand, and not the greatest of them. Let us dip our bucket into the well.

The tree of the knowledge of good and evil—that was the tree of morality! And morality was then the original sin? And through *it* Man lost his innocence? The antithesis of morality and innocence is as old as the world. And if we are to capture innocence again, if the world is to become æsthetically acceptable to us, we must dispense more and more with morality and limit its domain. This, one desperate glance into the depths of the myth tells us. Instinct is upheld in it against isolated reason and exterior law. Detached, "abstract" Reason brought sin into the world, but Instinct, which is fundamentally Love, Creation, Will to Power, is forever innocent, beyond good and evil. It was when Reason, no longer the sagacity of Instinct, no longer the eyes of Love, became its opponent and oppressor, that morality arose and Man fell.

Or to take another guess, granted we read Original Sin in the Fall, must we not read there, also, the way to get rid of it? If by Original Sin Man fell, then by renouncing it let him arise again. But how renounce it? What! Cannot Man renounce a metaphor?

Yet how powerful is metaphor! Man is ruled by metaphor. The gods were nothing but that, some sublime, some terrible, some lovely, all metaphors, Jehovah, Moloch, Apollo, Eros. Life is now stained through and through with metaphor. And there are further transfigurations still possible! Yet we would not destroy the beauty already starring Life's skies, the lovely hues lent by Aphrodite, and Artemis, and Dionysos, or the sublime colours of Jehovah and Thor. But the heavy disfiguring blot tarnishing all, Love, Innocence, Ecstasy, Wrath, that we would rather altogether extirpate and annul. Original Sin we would cut off as a disfigurement and disease of Life.

Or, again, may not the myth be an attempt to glorify Man and to clothe him with a sad splendour. And not Original Sin, but Original Innocence is the true reading of the fable? Its *raison d'être* is the Garden of Eden, not the Fall? To glorify Humanity at its source it set there a Superman. The fall from innocence—that was the fall from the Superman into Man.

And how, then, is Man to be redeemed? By the return of the Superman! Let that be our reading of the myth!

45

The Use of Myth

In the early world myth was used to dignify Man by idealizing his origin. Henceforward it must be used to dignify him by idealizing his goal. *That* is the task of the poets and artists.

46

Before the Fall

Innocence is the morality of the instincts. Original Sin—that was war upon the instincts, morality become abstract, separate, self-centred, accusing and tyrannical. This self-consciousness of morality, this disruption in the nature of Man, was the Fall.

47

Beyond Original Sin

How far is Man still from his goal? How sexual, foul in word and thought, naively hedonistic! How little of spirit is in him! How clumsily his mind struggles in the darkness! How far he is still from his goal!—This is a cry which the believer in Original Sin cannot understand, because he accepts all this imperfection as inevitable, as the baleful heritage of Man, from which he cannot escape.

The feeling of pure joy in life, the feeling that Life is a sacrament—that also is forever denied to the believer in Original Sin. For Life is not a sacrament to him, but a sin of which joy itself is only an aggravation.

48

The Eternal Bluestocking

The bluestocking is as old as mankind. Her original was Eve, the first dabbler in moral philosophy.

49

The Sin of Intellectualism

The first sin, the original sin was that of the intellectuals. The knowledge of Good and Evil was not an instantaneous "illumination"; it was the result of long experiment and analysis: the apple took perhaps hundreds of years to eat! Before that, in the happy day of innocence, Good and Evil were not, for instinct and morality were one and not twain. As time passed, however, the physically lazy, who had been from the beginning, became weaker and wiser. Enforced contemplation, the contemplation of those who were not strong enough to hunt or to labour, made them more subtle than their simple brethren; they formed themselves into a priesthood, and created a theology. In these priests instinct was not strong: they were invalids with powerful reason. But they had the lust for power; they wished to conquer by means of their reason; therefore, they said to themselves, belittle instinct, tyrannize over instinct, discover an absolute "good" and an absolute "evil," become moral. Morality, which had in the days of innocence been unconscious, the harmony of the instincts, was now given a separate existence. The cry was morality against the instincts. Thus triumphed the priests, the intellectuals, by means of their reason. Original Sin was their sin—the result of the analysis by which they had separated morality and the instincts. If we are to speak of Original Sin at all, let it be in this manner.

50

Once More

The belief in Original Sin—that was itself Man's original sin.

51

Apropos Gautier

He had just read "Mlle. de Maupin," "What seduction there is still for Man in the senses!" he exclaimed. "How much more of an animal than a spirit he must be to be charmed and enslaved by this book!" Yet, what ground had he to conclude that because the sensual intoxicates Man, therefore Man is more sensual than spiritual? For we are most fatally attracted by what is most alien to us.

52

Psychology of the Humble

There is something very naïve in those who speak of humility as a certain good and of pride as a proven evil. In the first place these are not opposites at all; there are a hundred kinds of both, and humility is sometimes simply a refined form of pride. Humility may be prudence, or good taste, or timidity, or a concealment, or a sermon, or a snub. How much of it, for instance, is simple prudence? Is not this, indeed, its chief *utility*, that it saves men from the dangers which accompany pride? On the day on which some one discovered that "Pride goeth before a fall," humility became no mean virtue. For if one become the servant and proclaim himself the least of all, how can he still fall? Yet if he does it is a fall into greater humility, and his virtue only shows the brighter. This is the sagacity of the humble, that they turn even ignominy to their glorification.

Humility is most commonly used with a different meaning, however. There are people who wish to be anonymous and uniform, and people who desire to be personal and distinct. Or, more exactly, it is their instincts that seek these ends. The first are humble in the fundamental sense that they are instinctively so; the latter are proud in the same sense. Humility, then, is the desire to be as others are and to escape notice; and this desire can only be realized in conformity. It is true, people become conceited after a while about their very conformity, and would be wounded in their vanity if they failed to comply with fashion; but vanity and humility are not incompatible.

Pride, however, is something much more subtle. The naïve, unconditional contemners of pride, who plead with men to cast it out, have certainly no idea what would happen if they were obeyed. For pride is the condition of all fruitful action. This thought must be consciously or subconsciously present in the doer, What I do is of value! I am capable of doing a thing which is worth doing! The Christian, it is true, still acts, though he is convinced that all action is sinful and of little worth. But it is only his mind that is convinced: his instincts are by no means persuaded of the truth of this! For though in the conscious there may be self-doubt, in the unconscious there *must* be pride, or actions would not be performed at all. Moreover, in all those qualities which are personal and not common—in personality—pride is an essential ingredient. The pronoun "I" is itself an affirmation of pride. The feeling, This is myself, this quality is *my* quality, by possessing it I am different from you, these things constitute *my* personality and *are* me: what a naïve assumption of the valuableness of these qualities do we have there, how much pride is there in that unconscious confession! And without this instinctive pride, these qualities, personality could never have been possible. In the heart of all distinct, valuable and heroic things, pride lies coiled. Yes, even in the heart of humility, of the most refined, spiritual humility. For such humility is *not* a conformity; it separates and individualizes its possessor as effectually as pride could; it takes its own path and not that of the crowd; and so its source must be in an inward sense of worth, of independence: it is a form of pride. But pride is so closely woven into life that to wound it is to wound life; to abolish it, if that were possible, would be to abolish life. Well do its subtler defamers know that! And when they shoot their arrows at pride, it is Life they hope to hit.

53

Les Humbles

Humility is the chief virtue, said a humble man. Then are you the vainest man, said his friend, for you are renowned for your humility. Good taste demands from writers who praise humility a little aggressiveness and dogmatism, lest they be taken for humble, and, therefore, proud. On the other hand, if humility is the chief virtue, it is immoral not to practise it. And, therefore, one should praise humility, and practise it? Or praise it and not practise it? Or not praise it and practise it? There is contradiction in every course. That is the worst of believing in paradoxical virtues!

54

Against the Ostentatiously Humble

He who is truly humble conceals even his humility.

55

The Pessimists

In pessimistic valuations of Life, the alternative contemplated is generally not between Life and Death, but between different types of Life. The real goal of Schopenhauerism is not the extinction of life, for death is a perfectly normal aspect of existence, and Life would not be denied even if death became universal. In order to deny Life and to triumph over it, the pessimist must continue at least to exist, in a sort of death in life: he must be dead, but he must also know it. That is the goal of Schopenhauerism; perhaps not so difficult, perhaps frequently attained! "They have not enough life even to die," said Nietzsche.

56

Sickness and Health

Some men have such unconquerable faith in Life that they defy their very maladies, creating out of them forms of ecstasy: that is their way of triumphing over them. Perhaps some poetry, certainly not a little religion has sprung from this. In religions defaming the senses and enjoining asceticism, or, in other words, a lowering of vitality, the chronic sufferers *affirm* Life in their own way; for sickness *is* their life: their praise of sickness is their praise of Life. And if they sometimes morbidly invite death, that is because death is nothing but another form of experience, of Life. To the sick, if they are to retain self-respect and pride, these doctrines are perhaps the best possible; it is only to the healthy that they are noxious. For the healthy who are converted by them, become sick through them, yet not so sick as to find comfort in them. The aspiration after an ascetic life contends in these men with their old health, their desire to live fully, and causes untold perplexities and conflicts; leaving them at last with nothing but a despairing desire for release. Thus, a religion of consolation becomes for the strong a Will to Death—the very opposite of that which it was to those who created it.

57

The Pride of the Sterile

Ecclesiastical, ceremonious humility is the pride of those who cannot create or initiate, either because they are sterile, or because the obstacles in their way are too great. Their pride is centred, not on what they can do, but on what they can endure. The anchorite goes into the wilderness, perhaps rather to get his background than to escape attention, and there imposes upon himself the most difficult and loathsome tasks, enduring not only outward penances, fasting and goading of the flesh, but such inward convulsions, portents and horrors, as the soul of man has by no other means experienced. Here, in endurance, is his power, and here, therefore, is his pride: the poor Atlas, who does not remove, but supports mountains, and these of his own making!

Men who have the power to create but are at the same time extremely timid belong to this class. Rather than venture outside themselves they will do violence to their own nature. The forces which in creation would have been liberated are pent within them and cause untold restlessness, uneasiness and pain. Religions which stigmatize "self-expression," separating the individual into an "outward" and an "inward" and raising a barrier between the two, encourage the growth of this type of man. These religions themselves have their roots in a timidity, a fear of pain. For self-expression is by no means painless; it is, on the contrary, a great cause of suffering. Essentially its outcome is strife, the clash of egos: Tragedy is the great recognition in Art of this truth. Christianity saw the suffering which conflict brought with it, said it was altogether evil, and sought to abolish it. But a law of Life cannot be abolished: strife, driven from the world of outward event, retreated into the very core of man, and there became baleful, indeed, disintegrating, and subversive. The early Christians did not see that men would suffer more from that inward psychic conflict than from the other. It was the Greeks who elevated conflict to an honourable position in their outward actions; with them, as Nietzsche said, there was no distinction between the "outward" and "inward"; they lived completely and died once. But the Christians, to use the words of St. Paul, "died daily." How true was that of those proudly humble anchorites! What a light it throws upon their sternly endured convulsions of the soul! In the end, Death itself came no doubt to many of them as a relief from this terribly protracted "dying." Perhaps one thing, however, made their lives bearable and even enjoyable—the power of the soul to plumb its own sufferings and capacity for endurance. Psychology arose first among the ecclesiastically humble men.

Well, let us count up our gains and losses. Spiritual humility, wherever it has spread, has certainly weakened the expression of Life: for it has weakened man by introducing within him a disrupting conflict. But it has also made Life subtler and deeper; it has enlarged the inward world of man, even if it has straitened the world outside. So that when we return—as we must—to the Pagan ideal of "expression," our works shall be richer than those of the Pagans, for man has now *more* to express.

58

When Pride is Necessary

Perhaps in all great undertakings into which uncertainty enters pride is necessary. In the Elizabethan age, our most productive and adventurous age, pride was at its zenith. Was that pride the necessary condition of that productiveness? Would the poets, the thinkers and the discoverers have attempted what they did attempt, had they been humble men? What is needed is more enquiry: a new psychology, and, above all, a new history of pride.

59

Humility and the Artists

There is one man, at any rate, who has always owed more to pride than to humility—the artist. Whether it be in himself, where it is almost the condition of productiveness, or in others, where it is the cause of all actions and movements æsthetically agreeable, Pride is his great benefactor. All artists are proud, but not all have the good conscience of their pride. In their thoughts they permit themselves to be persuaded too much by the theologians; they have not enough "free spirit" to say, "Pride is my atmosphere, in which I create. I do not choose to refuse my atmosphere."

But if pride were banished even from the remainder of Life, how poor would the artists be left! For every gesture that is beautiful, all free, spirited, swift movement and all noble repose have in them pride. Humility uglifies, except, indeed, the humility which is a form of pride; that has a sublimity of its own. Even the Christian Church—the Church of the humble—had to make its ceremonies magnificent to make itself æsthetically presentable; without its magnificence it would have been an impossible institution. Humility, to be supportable, must have in it an admixture of pride. That gives it *standing*. It was His subtle pride that communicated to the humility of Jesus its gracious "charm."

Poetic tragedy and pride are profoundly associated. No event is tragic which has not arisen out of pride, and has not been borne proudly: the Greeks knew that. But, as well, is not pride at times laughable and absurd? Well, what does that prove, except that comedy as well as tragedy has been occasioned by it? Humility is not even laughable!

60

Love and Pride

Pride is so indissolubly bound up with everything great—Joy, Beauty, Courage, Creation—that surely it must have had some celestial origin. Who created it? Was it Love, who wished to shape a weapon for itself, the better to fashion things? Pride has so much to do with creation that sometimes it imagines it is a creator. But that it is not. Only Love can create. Pride was fashioned out of a rib taken from the side of Love.

61

Pride and the Fall

It was not humility that was the parent of the fable of the Fall. Or is it humility to boast of one's high ancestry, and if the ancestry does not exist, to invent it? The naïve poet who created that old allegory did not foresee the number of interpretations which would be read into it. He did not foresee that it would be used to humiliate Man instead of to exalt him; he did not at all foresee Original Sin. As less than justice, then, has been meted to him, let us now accord him more than justice. Let us say that he was a divine philosopher who perceived that in unconditional morality lay the grand misfortune of mankind. Man is innocent; thus, he said, it is an absolute ethic that defiles him—the knowledge of Good and Evil. Sweep that away, and he is innocent and back in the Garden of Eden again. Let us say this of the first poet, for certainly he did not mean it! Perhaps he knew nothing at all about morality! All that he wished for was to provide a dignified family tree for his generation.

62

The Good Conscience

What a revolution for mankind it would be to get back "the good conscience"? Life made innocent, washed free from how much filth of remorse, guilt, contempt, "sin"—that vision arouses a longing more intense than that of the religious for any heaven. And it seems at least equally possible of realization! Bad conscience arises when religion and the instincts are in opposition; the more comprehensive and deep this conflict, the more guilty the conscience. But there have been religions not antagonistic to the instincts, which, instead of condemning them, have thought so well of them as to become their rule, their discipline. The religion of the Greeks was an example of this; and in Greece, accordingly, there was no "bad conscience" in our sense. Well, how is it possible, if it *is* possible, to regain "the good conscience"? Not by any miracle! Not by an instantaneous "change of heart," for even the heart changes slowly. But suppose that a new instinctive religion and morality were to be set up, and painfully complied with, until they became a second nature as ours have become, should we not then gradually lose our bad conscience, born as it is out of the antagonism between instinct and morality? Nay, if we were to persevere still further until instinct and religion and morality became intermingled and indistinguishable, might we not enter the Garden of Eden again, might not innocence itself become ours? But to attain that end, an unremitting discipline, extending over hundreds of years, might be necessary; and who, in the absence of gods, is to impose that discipline?

63

The Other Side

The life-defaming creeds are not to be condemned unconditionally: even they are not evil. "Guilt," asceticism, contempt for the world—these are the physiologically bad things which have sharpened, deepened and made subtle the soul of man. The Greeks were simple compared with modern man; a thousand times more healthy, it is true—perhaps because they were incapable of contracting our maladies. Well, let us judge Christianity, which in Europe was mainly responsible for this deepening of Man, by an artistic criterion: let us judge it by the effects it achieved, not by what it said.

64

Effects of Christianity

If there are gods who take an interest in Man, and experiment upon him, what better means could they have devised for getting out of him certain "effects," not Christian at all, than Christianity? Far more significant for mankind than the virtues of Christianity, are its contradictions, excesses and "states of mind." The "way of life," Christian morality, is of little account compared with the permanent physiological and psychological transformations effected upon Man by the discipline of centuries of religion. Not that Man has been forced into the mould of Christian morality, but that in the process he has undergone the most unique convulsions, adaptations and permutations, that an entire new world of conflict, pain, fear, horror, exaltation, faith and scepticism has been born within him, that Life, driven within itself, has deepened, enriched and invested him—*that* is from the standpoint of human culture the most important thing, beside which what is usually understood by the Christianizing of Europe is relatively insignificant. Not Christian morality, but the effects of Christian morality it is that now concern us. And these effects are not themselves Christian; rather the contrary. Christianity has made Man more complex, contradictory, sceptical, tragic and sublime; it has given him more capacity for good and for evil, and has added to these two qualities subtlety and spirituality.

III
WHAT IS MODERN?

65

Whither?

The fever of modern thought which burns in our veins, and from which we refuse to escape by reactionary backdoors—Christianity and the like—is not without its distinction: it is an "honourable sickness," to use the phrase of Nietzsche. I speak of those who sincerely strive to seek an issue from this fever; to pass through it into a new health. Of the others to whom fever is the condition of existence, who make a profession of their maladies, the valetudinarians of the spirit, the dabblers in quack soul-remedies for their own sake, it is impossible to speak without disdain. Our duty is to exterminate them, by ridicule or any other means found effectual. But we are ourselves already too grievously harassed; we are caught in the whirlwind of modern thought, which contains as much dust as wind. We see outside our field of conflict a region of Christian calm, but never, never, never can we return there, for our instincts as well as our intellect are averse to it. The problem must have a different solution. And what, indeed, is the problem? To some of us it is still that of emancipation—that which confronted Goethe, Ibsen, Nietzsche, and the other great spirits of last century. It is an error to think that these men have yet been refuted or even understood; they have simply been buried beneath the corpses of later writers. And it is the worst intellectual weakness, and, therefore, crime of our age that ideas are no longer disproved, but simply superseded by newer ideas. The latest is the true, and Time refutes everything! That is our modern superstition. We have still, then, to go back—or, rather, forward—to Goethe, Ibsen and Nietzsche. Our problem is still that of clearing a domain of freedom around us, of enlarging our field of choice, and so making destiny itself more spacious; and, then, having delivered ourselves from prejudice and superstition—and how many other things!—of setting an aim before us for the unflinching pursuit of which we make ourselves responsible.

Greater freedom, and therefore greater responsibility, above all greater aims, an enlargement of life, not a whittling of it down to Christian standards—that is our problem still!

66

The "Restoration" of Christianity

Will Christianity ever be established again? It is doubtful. At the most, it may be "restored"—in the manner of the architectural "restorations," against which Ruskin declaimed. The difficulty of re-establishing it must needs be greater than that of establishing it. For it has now been battered by science (people no longer believe in miracles) and by history (people have read what the Church has done—or has not done). Christianity has become a Church, and the Church, an object of criticism. As the body which housed the spirit of Christianity, men have studied it with secular eyes, and have found little to reverence, much to censure; and in the disrepute into which the body has fallen, the spirit, also, has shared. And now the atmosphere cannot be created in which Christianity may grow young again and recapture its faith. The necessary credulity, or, at any rate, the proper kind of credulity, is no longer ours. For Christianity grew, like the mushrooms, *in the night*. Had there been newspapers in Judea, there had been no Christianity. And this age of ours, in which the clank of the printing press drowns all other sounds, is fatal to any noble mystery, to any noble birth or rebirth. *That* night, at all events, we can never pass through again, and, therefore, Christianity will probably never renew itself.

67

A Drug for Diseased Souls

The utmost that can be expected is a "restoration," and in that direction we have gone already a long way. For Christianity is not now, as it was at the beginning, a spring of inspiration, a thing spiritual, spontaneous, Dionysian. It is mainly a remedy, or, more often, a drug for diseased souls; and, therefore, to be husbanded strictly by the modern medicine men, to be dispensed carefully, and, yes, to be advertised as well! Its birth was out of an exuberance of spiritual life; its "restoration" will be out of a hopeless debility and fatigue. And, therefore—

68

The Dogmatists

All religions may be regarded from two sides; from that of their creators, and from that of their followers. Among the creators are to be numbered not only the founders of religion, but the saints, the inspired prophets and every one who has in some degree the genius for religion. They are not distinguished by much reverence for dogma, but by the "religious feeling"; and when this emotion carries them away in its flood they often treat dogma in a way to make the orthodox gape with horror. But, in truth, they do not themselves take much account of dogma; every dogma is a crutch, and they do not feel the need of one. But the people who are not sustained by this inward spring of emotion, who can never know what religion really is, these need a crutch; it is for them that dogma was designed. And, of course, the real religious men see their advantage also in the adherence of the dogmatists, the many; for the more widely a religion is spread, the more secure it becomes, and the greater chance it has of enduring. Dogma, then, is religion for the irreligious. To the saint religion is a thing inward and creative; to the dogmatist it is a thing outward, accomplished and fixed, to which he may cling. The former is the missionary of religion, the latter, its conserver. The one is religious because he has religion, the other, because he needs it.

69

The Religious Impulse

The time comes in the history of a faith when the "religious feeling" dies, and nothing is left but dogma. The dogmatists then become the missionaries of religion. The fount is dried up; there is no longer an inward force seeking for expression; there is only the fear of the dogmatist lest his staff, his guide, his horizon should be taken from him. Religion is then supported most frenziedly by the irreligious; weakness then speaks with a more poignant eloquence than strength itself. And that is what is happening with Christianity. Its "religious feeling" is dead: there has been no great religious figure in Europe in our time. And the Church is now being defended on grounds neither religious nor theological, but secular and even utilitarian. The real religious impulse is now to be found in the movement outside, and, *therefore*, against Christianity. But, alas, as Nietzsche feared, there may not after all be "sufficient religion in the world to destroy religion."

70

The Decay of Prophecy

The past should be studied only in order to divine the future. The new soothsayers should seek for omens, not, as their ancient brethren did, in the stars and the entrails of animals, but in the book of history, past and becoming. "The new soothsayers," for soothsaying has not died; it has become popular—and degenerate. Every one may now foretell the future, but no one may believe what is foretold. And that is because the soothsayers do not themselves believe their auguries; when they happen to speak the truth, no one is more surprised than they. But in the antique world the augurs had, at any rate, responsibility; to foretell the future was not to them an amusement but a vocation.

To what is due the decay of the art of soothsaying? Partly, no doubt, to the dissemination of popular knowledge, by which people have become less credulous; partly to the "scientific temper" of those who, had they lived in the old world, would have been the soothsayers; partly to other causes known to every one. But, allowing for these, may there not be *something* due to the fact that people are no longer interested, as they used to be, in the future? They know the past, ah, perhaps too well: they have looked into it so long that at length they feel that the future holds nothing which it has not held, that Fate has now no fresh metamorphosis or apotheosis, and that Time must henceforth be content to plagiarize itself. And so the future has lost the seduction which it once held for the noblest spirits. It is true, men still amuse themselves by guessing which of Time's well-thumbed and greasy cards will turn up at the next deal, or by playing at patience with the immemorial possibilities. But that is not soothsaying, nor is it even playing with the future: it is playing with the past. And the great modern discovery is not the discovery of the future, but the discovery of the past.

And as with soothsaying, so with prophecy. If we could but look for a moment into the soul of an old prophet and see his deepest thoughts and visions, what a conception of the future would be ours! But that is impossible. We cannot now understand the faith of the men who, unmoved, prophesied the advent of supernatural beings, the Christ or another; to whom the future was a new world more strange than America was to Columbus. That attitude of mind has been killed; and now comes one who says the belief in the future is a weakness. Would he, perchance, have said that to John the Baptist, the great modern of his time? Had he lived in that pre-Christian world, would he have believed in the God in whom he now believes? The orthodox Christian here finds himself in a laughable dilemma. Admitting nothing wonderful in the future, he is yet constrained to believe in a past wonderful beyond the dreams of poets or of madmen—a past in which supernatural beings, miracles and portents were almost the rule. And so the future is to him not even so wonderful as the past. It is an expurgated edition of the past—an edition with the incidents and marvels left out, a novel without a hero or a plot.

So, for good or for evil, we no longer believe in the future as we did: it is steadily becoming less marvellous, and, therefore, less seductive for us. But, without the bait of the strange and the new to lure it on, must not humanity halt on its way? *Can* man act at all without believing in the future in some fashion? Must not things be *foreseen* before they can be accomplished? Is not soothsaying implicit in every deliberate act? Are not all sincere ideals involuntary auguries? Is it not the future rather than the prophecy which "comes true"? Did not the old prophecies "come true" *because* they were prophesied? Did not Christ arise *because* He was foretold? And are not the believers in the future, then, the creators of the future, and the true priests of progress? When we can envisage a future noble enough, it will not then be weakness to believe in it.

71

The Great Immoralists

The morality of Nietzsche is more strict and exacting than that of Christianity. When the Christians argue against it, therefore, they are arguing in favour of a morality more comfortable, pleasing and indulgent to the natural man; consequently, even on religious grounds, of a morality more immoral. What! is Nietzsche, then, the great moralist, and are the Christians the great immoralists?

This notion may appear to us absurd, or merely ingenious, but will it appear so to future generations? Will timidity, conformity, mediocrity, judicious blindness, unwillingness to offend, be synonymous, to them also, with morality? Or will they look back upon Christianity as a creed too indulgent and not noble enough? As a sort of Epicureanism, for instance?

72

The First and the Last

We all know what the weak have suffered from the strong; but who shall compute what the strong have suffered from the weak?" The last shall be first"; but when they become first they become also the worst tyrants—impalpable, anonymous and petty.

73

Humility in Pride

The pride of some gifted men is not pride in their person, but in something within them, of which they regard themselves the guardians and servants. If there is dignity in their demeanour it is a reflected, impersonal dignity. Just so a peasant might feel ennobled who guarded a king in danger and exile.

74

The Modern Devil

The devil is not wicked but corrupt, in modern phraseology, decadent. The qualities of the mediæval devil, rage, cruelty, hatred, pride, avarice, are in their measure necessary to Life, necessary to virtue itself. But corruption is wholly bad; it contaminates even those who fight it. Hell relaxes: Mr. Shaw's conception is profoundly true.

But if the devil is corruption, cannot the devil be abolished? It is true, Man cannot extirpate cruelty, hatred and pride without destroying Life; but Life is made more powerful by the destruction of the corrupt. God created Man; but it was Man that created the devil.

75

Master and Servant

To summon out of the void a task, and then incontinently to make of himself its slave: that is the happiness of many a man. A great means of happiness!

76

Criterions

It is not expedient to choose on *every* occasion the higher rather than the lower, for one may not be able to endure too much living on the heights. If will and capacity were always equal! Then, it is true, there would not be any difficulty; but Life is Life, after all—that is, our will *is* greater than our capacity. On the other hand, it is not well to develop equally all our faculties—the formula of the Humanist—for among them there is a hierarchy, and some are more worthy of development than others. What course is left? To act always in the interest of what is highest in us, and when we partake of a lower pleasure to regard it as a form of sleep, of necessary forgetting? For even the mind must slumber occasionally if it is to remain healthy.

77

Intellectual Prudence

Among athletes there is a thing known as over-training: if it is persisted in it wrecks the body. A similar phenomenon is to be found among thinkers: thought too severe and protracted may ruin the mind. Was this the explanation of Nietzsche's downfall? Certainly, his intellectual health was that of the athlete who remains vigorous by virtue of a never-sleeping discipline, who maintains his balance by a continuous effort. This is perhaps the highest, the most exquisite form of health, but it is at the same time the most dangerous—a little more, a little less, and the engine of thought is destroyed. It is important that the thinker should discover exactly how far he may discipline himself, and how far permit indulgence. What in the ordinary man—conscious of no *secondary raison d'être*—is performed without fuss by the instincts, must by him be *thought out*—a task of great peril.

78

A Dilemma

To be a man is easy: to be a purpose is more difficult; but, on the whole—easy. In the first instance, one has but to exist; in the second, to act. But to unite man and purpose in the same person—to be a type—is both difficult and precarious. For that a balance is imperative: "being" and "doing" must be prevented from injuring each other: action must become rhythm, and rest, a form of energy. To be in doing, to do in being—that is the task of the future man. The danger of our being mere man is that mankind may remain forever stationary, without a goal. The danger of our being mere purpose is that our humanity may altogether drop out and nothing but the purpose be left. And would not that defeat the purpose?

79

Dangers of Genius

Why is it that so many men of genius have been destroyed by falling into chasms of desire which are safely trodden by common men? Is it because there is within the exceptional man greater compass, and, therefore, greater danger? The genius has left the animal further behind than the ordinary man; indeed, in the genius of the nobler sort there is an almost passionate avoidance and disavowal of the animal. In this disavowal lie at once his safety and his danger: by means of it he climbs to perilous heights, and is also secure upon them. But let him abrogate even once this denial of kinship, and he is in the utmost danger. He now finds himself stationed on the edge of a precipice up to which he seems to have climbed in a dream, a dreadful dizziness assails him, along with a mad desire to fling himself into the depths. It was perhaps a leap of this kind that Marlowe made, and Shelley. Meantime, the ordinary man lives in safety at the foot of the precipice: he is never so far above the animal as to be injured by a fall into animalism. Only to the noble does spiritual *danger* come.

80

A Strange Failure

He failed; for the task was too *small* for him—a common tale among men of genius. You have been unsuccessful in trivial things? There is always a remedy left: to essay the great. How often has Man become impotent simply because there was no task heroic enough to demand greatness of him!

81

Dangers of the Spiritual

If you are *swept off your feet* by a strongly sensuous book, it is probably a sign that you have become too highly spiritualized. For a sensualist would simply have enjoyed it, while feeling, perhaps, a little bored and dissatisfied. It was only a religious anchorite who could have lost his *soul* to Anatole France's Thaïs. For the salvation of Man it is more than ever imperative that a reconciliation should be effected between the spirit and the senses. Until it is, the highest men—the most spiritual—will be in the very greatest peril, and will almost inevitably be wrecked or frustrated. It is for the good of the *soul* that this reconciliation must now be sought.

82

Again

From the diabolization of the senses innumerable evils have flowed; physical and mental disease, disgust with the world, cruelty towards everything natural. But, worst of all, it has made sensuality a greater *danger* than it was ever before. In the anchorite, seeking to live entirely in the spirit, and ignoring or chastising the body, sensuality was driven into the very soul, and there was magnified a hundredfold. To the thinker avoiding the senses as much as possible—for he had been taught to distrust them—sensuality, in the moments when he was brought face to face with it, had acquired a unique seductiveness, and had become a problem and a danger. If he yielded, it was perilous in a degree unknown to the average sensual man; if he resisted, a good half of his spiritual energy was wasted in keeping the senses at bay. In either case, the thinker suffered. So that now it is the spirit that has become the champion of the senses, but for the good of the spirit.

83

God and Animal

Until the marriage of the soul and the senses has been accomplished, Man cannot manifest himself in any *new* type. What has been the history of humanity during the last two thousand years? The history of humanity, that is, as distinct from the history of communities? A record of antithetic tyrannies, the spiritual alternating with the sensual; an uncertain tussle between God and animal, now one uppermost, now the other; not a tragedy—for in Tragedy there is significance—but a gloomy farce. And this farce must continue so long as the spirit contems sense as evil in itself—for neither of them can be abolished! Whether we like it or not, the senses, so long as they are oppressed and defamed, will continue to break out in terrible insurrections of sensuality and excess, until, tired and satiated, they return again under the tyranny of the spirit—at the appointed time, however, to revolt once more. From this double *cul de sac* Man can be freed only by a reconciliation between the two. When this happens, however, it will be the beginning of a higher era in the history of humanity; Man will then become spiritual in a new sense. Spirit will then affirm Life, instead of, as now, slandering it; existence will become joyful and tragic; for to live in accordance with Life itself—voluntarily to approve struggle, suffering and change—is the most difficult and heroic of lives. The softening of the rigour of existence, its reduction and weakening by asceticism, humility, "sin," is the *easier* path; *narrow* is the way that leads to Nihilism! The error of Heine was that he prophesied a *happier* future from the reconciliation of the body and the soul: his belief in the efficacy of happiness was excessive. But this reconciliation is, nevertheless, of importance for *nothing else* than its *spiritual* significance: by means of it Man is freed from his labyrinth, and can at last *move forward*—he becomes more tragic.

84

Ultimate Pessimism

To the most modern man must have come at some time the thought, What if this thing spirit be *essentially* the enemy of the senses? What if, like the vampire, it *can* live only by drinking blood? What if the conflict between spirit and "life" is and must forever be an implacable and destructive one? He is then for a moment a Christian, but with an added bitterness which few Christians have known. For if his thought be true, then the weakening and final nullification of Life must be our object.

To prove that the spirit and the senses are not eternally irreconcilable enemies is still a task. Those who believe they are, do so as an act of faith: their opponents are in the same case. We should never cease to read spirit into Life-affirming things, such as pride, heroism and love, and to magnify and exalt these aspects of the spirit.

85

Leisure and Productiveness

Granted that the society which produces the highest goods in the greatest profusion is the best—let us not argue from this that society should be organized with the direct aim of producing goods. For what if goods be to society what happiness is said to be to men—things to be attained only by striving for something else? In all good things—whether it be in art, literature or philosophy—there is much of the free, the perverse, the unique, the incalculable. In short, good things can only be produced by great men—and these are exceptions. The best we can do, then, is to inaugurate a society in which great men will find it possible to live, will be even encouraged to live. Can a society in which rights are affixed to functions serve for that? A function, in practice, in a democratic state—that will mean something which can be seen to be useful for today, but not for tomorrow, far less for any distant future. The more subtle, spiritual, posthumous the activity of a man the less it will be seen to be a function. Art and philosophy arise when leisure and not work is the ruling convention. It is true that artists and philosophers work, and at a higher tension than other men; but it is in leisure that they must *conceive* their works: what obvious function do they then fulfil? Even the most harassed of geniuses, even Burns would never have become immortal had he not had the leisure to ponder, dream and love. Idleness is as necessary for the production of a work of art as labour. And with some men perhaps whole years of idleness are needed. Artists must always be privileged creatures. It is privileges, and not rights, that they want.

86

What is Freedom?

The athlete, by the disciplining of his body, creates for himself a new world of actions; he can now do things which before were prohibited to him; in consequence, he has enlarged the sphere of his freedom. The thinker and the artist by discipline of a different kind are rewarded in the same way. They are now more free, because they have now more capacity.

There are people, however, who think one can be free whether one has the capacity for freedom or not—a characteristically modern fallacy. But a man the muscles of whose body and mind are weak cannot do *anything;* how can he be free? The concept of Freedom cannot be separated from that of Power.

87

Freedom, in the Dance

Even the most unbridled dance is a form of constraint. The completest freedom of movement is the reward of the severest discipline.

88

A Moral for Moderns

A spring gushed forth here on the airy height; but the soil was not hard enough to retain it; and the water sapped away among the soft moss. One day a man came and laid down a hard channel for the spring. Imprisoned on both sides, it now imperiously sought an outlet and—a miracle!—leapt glittering into the sunshine. The history of Freedom.

89

The Renaissance: A Thesis

How unsatisfactory are those explanations of the Renaissance which give as its cause the breaking up of the restrictive intellectual canons of the Middle Ages—as if a mere negation could explain such a unique creative era! What has here to be discovered is how freedom and the *capacity* for freedom should have appeared at the same moment. Perhaps the Middle Ages have now been sufficiently reviled by the admirers of the Renaissance; perhaps that event owed more than we are willing to acknowledge to the centuries of mediæval repression and discipline. During these centuries the human spirit had been confined in the granite channel cut for it by mediæval Christianity, a channel of which even the mouth was stopped. In the fifteenth century the stream swept away every obstacle and leapt forth, a brilliant cascade, scattering almost pagan warmth and light. The fall of Constantinople and the other circumstances usually given as the explanation of this outburst were only its occasion; the cause lay much deeper, in the long storing up, conserving and strengthening of human powers. The freedom of which the Renaissance was an expression was more, then, than the simple removal of restriction. It was a freedom not political or moral, but vital; a positive enhancement if the natural power of man, who could now do things which hitherto he could not do—an event in the history, not merely of society, but of Man. Accordingly, the "freedom of the individual," so dear to some moderns, does not teach us much here. It was not because freedom was given to them that men now created: the freedom was claimed because they now possessed more power, could do more, and had, therefore, the *right* to a larger sphere of freedom. The more naturally free—that is, individually powerful—a people become, the more they will demand and obtain of "individual freedom"; but it is perhaps inexpedient to offer to a people individually weak any more freedom than they can use. They are still at the disciplinary stage; they are preparing for their renaissance; and to the student of human culture the periods of preparation, of unproductiveness, are more worthy of consideration than the productive periods. For in the future we must prepare for our eras of fruition, and not leave them, as in the past, to pure chance.

At the Renaissance, however, it was not even individual freedom in the modern democratic sense that was claimed and allowed; it was at the most the freedom of certain individuals, the naturally free, the powerful. Not until a later time was this claim to be universalized by the unconditional theorists, the generalizers *sans* distinction, the egalitarians. The French Revolution was the Renaissance rationalized and popularized.

90

The Unproductive Periods

Without the Middle Ages the Renaissance would have been impossible; the one, therefore, was as necessary as the other; and our reprobation of the former for its comparative sterility is entirely without justification. If we happen to be living in an unproductive age, it is our misfortune, then; but we are not entitled, in contemplating this age, to the luxury of condemnation, reproof or scorn. What we *may* demand of any period now is that it should be a period either of preparation or of fruition. So the present era *is*, after all, deserving of condemnation, but only because it is not an era of preparation—not for any other reason.

91

Duties of the Unproductive

The history of culture is the history of long ages of unproductiveness broken by short eras of production; but unproductiveness is the rule. The men born in barren periods have not, then, the right to bewail their lot: *we* have not that right. But what is of the first importance, for the sake of culture, is to find out what are the duties proper to men in a sterile age. Certainly their duty it is not to produce whether they are productive or not; that can only result in abortions and painful caricatures: does not contemporary literature demonstrate it? The work that is born out of the poverty of the artist is, as Nietzsche pointed out, decadent work, and debases the spectator, lowers his vitality.

What, then, are the tasks of a writer in an unproductive age? To live sparely and conserve strength? To make discipline more rigid? To preserve and fortify the tradition of culture? To render more accessible the sources from which creative literature draws its life, so that the *next* generation may be better placed? To observe vigilantly the signs of today—and not only of today? It may be so; but, also, when necessary, to throw these prudent and preservative tasks to the winds and spend his last ounce of strength in battling with the demons who make a productive era forever impossible. Yes, this last duty is for us today—the most important. And, we may depend, it is the creators—those who produce what they should not—who will fight most bitterly on the opposite side.

92

"Emancipation"

The rallying cry of the great writers of the last century was "emancipation." Goethe, Heine and Ibsen alike professed as their task the emancipation of man; Nietzsche, their successor, elevated the freed man, the Superman, into an ideal, in the pursuit of which it was necessary meantime that men should discipline themselves. The later moderns, our own contemporaries, have belittled this freedom, seeing in it nothing but a negation, the freedom *from* some one thing or another. But Ibsen and Heine, these men of true genius, who believed most sincerely that they were "brave soldiers in the war of the liberation of humanity" did not perhaps waste their powers in battling for a thing so trivial! It is barely possible that they meant by emancipation something much more profound; something spiritual and positive; indeed, nothing less than an enhancement of the powers of man! Certainly both poets looked forward to new "developments" of man: Heine with his "happier and more perfect generations, begot in free and voluntary embraces, blossoming forth in a religion of joy"; Ibsen with his perplexed figures painfully "working their way out to

Freedom." It was the task of us in this generation, who should have been the heirs of this tradition, but are not, to supply the commentary to this noble vision, to carry forward this religion of hope further and further. But the *cult* of modernity has itself prevented this; the latest theory has always seized us and exacted our belief for its hour; the present has invariably triumphed; and we have discarded the great work of last century before we have understood it. Heine has been seized mainly by the decadents; his healthy and noble sensuousness, his desire to restore the harmony between the senses and the soul, *as a means* towards the emancipation of man, and as nothing else, has been perverted by them into worship of the senses for their own sake—a thing which to Heine would have seemed despicable. Ibsen has fallen among the realists and propagandists; all the spiritual value of his work has for this age been lost—and what a loss!—his battle to deliver man from his weakness and inward slavery has been reduced —it is no exaggeration—to a battle to deliver the women of the middle classes from their husbands. The old story of emanation has been again repeated, with the distinction that here there is no trace left of the original source except negative ones! Well, we have to turn back again, our task, second to none in grandeur, before which we may well feel abashed, is still the same as that of Goethe, Ibsen and Nietzsche, the task of emancipation. To restore dignity to literature, indeed, it would be necessary to create such a task if it did not already exist.

93

Genealogy of the Moderns

This is what has happened. The conventional moderns of our time are the descendants *not* of Heine and Ibsen, but of the race against which the poets fought. They live unthinkingly in the present, just as their spiritual ancestors lived unthinkingly in the past. But slavery to the past has long ago fallen into the second place among dangers to humanity: it is slavery to the present that is now by far the greatest peril. Not because they broke the tyranny of the past, but because they had an ideal in the future are the great fighters of last century significant. To think of them as iconoclasts is to mistake for their aim the form of their activity: the past lay between them and their object: on that account alone did they destroy it. But the great obstacle now is the domination of the present; and were the demi-gods of last century alive today, they would be fighting precisely against *you*, my dear moderns, who live so complacently in your provincial present, making of it almost a cult. To be a modern in the true sense, however, is to be a fore-runner; there is in this age, an age of preparation, no other test of the modern. To believe that there are still potentialities in man; to have faith that the "elevation of the type Man" is possible, yes, that the time is ripe to prepare for it; and to write and live in and by that thought: this is to be modern.

94

Domination of the Present

To be modern in the accepted, intellectually fashionable sense: what is that? To propagate always the newest theory, whatever it be; to be the least possible distance behind the times, behind the latest second of the times, whether they be good or bad; and, of course, to assume one is "in the circle" and to adopt the tone of the circle: in short, to make ideas a matter of fashion, to choose views as a well-to-do woman chooses dresses—to be intellectually without foundation, principles or taste. How did this convention arise? Perhaps out of lack of leisure: superficiality is bound to engulf a generation who abandon leisure. But to be enslaved to the present in this way is the most *dangerous* form of superficiality: it is to be ignorant of the very thing that makes Man significant, and with idiotic cheerfulness and unconcern to render his existence meaningless and trivial. In two ways' can Man become sublime; by regarding himself as the heir of a great tradition: by making of himself a fore-runner. Both ways are open to the true modern, and both must be followed by him. For the past and the future are greater than the present: the sense of continuity is necessary for human dignity.

The men of this age, however, are isolated—to use an electrical metaphor—from the current of Humanity: they have become almost entirely individuals, temporal units, "men"; what has been the outcome? Inevitably the loss of the concept Man, for Man is a concept which can be understood only through the contemplation on a grand scale of the history of mankind. Man ceases to be dramatic when there are no longer spectators for the drama of Humanity. The present generation have, therefore, no sentiment of the human sublime; they see that part of the grand tragedy which happens to pass before them, but without caring about what went before or what will come after, without a clue, however poor, to the mystery of existence. They know men only, the men of their time. They are provincial—that is, lacking the sentiment of Man.

How much decadence may not be traced to this! In Art, the conventions of Realism and of Æstheticism have arisen. The first is just the portrayal of present-day men *as* present-day men; nothing more, therefore, than "contemporary art"; an appendage of the present, a triviality. The second has as its creed enjoyment of the moment; and if it contemplates the past at all, it is with the eyes of the voluptuous antiquary—but a collector is not an heir. Art has in our time, both in theory and in practice, become deliberately more fleeting. In morality, there is Humanitarianism, or, in other words, the conviction that the suffering of today is the most important thing, coupled with the belief that there is nothing at present existing which can justify and redeem this suffering: therefore, unconditional pity, alleviation, "the greatest happiness of the greatest number." Modern pessimism, which springs from the same source, is the obverse of this belief. It, also, regards only the present, and says, perhaps with truth, that *it*, at any rate, is not noble enough to deserve and demand the suffering necessary for its existence—consequently, *all life* is an error! All these theories, however, are breaks with the spiritual tradition of emancipation; they are founded on the magnification of the temporary—of that which only in a present continually carried forward seems to be important. This judgment of Life with the eyes of the present, this narrowest and most false of interpretations: how has it confused and finally stultified the finest talents of our time! The modern man is joyless; his joylessness has arisen out of his modernity; and now to find forgetfulness of it he plunges more madly than before—into modernity! For his own sake, as much as for that of Humanity, it is our duty to free him from his wheel. One can live with dignity only if one have a sense of the tragedy of Man. It is the first task of the true modern to destroy the domination of the present.

95

Encyclopædists

Strange that the great dramatic poets of modern times have had a weakness for turning their tragedies into encyclopædias! Consider "Faust" and "Brand," for instance. Is it that the sentiment of the eternal was already beginning to weaken in Goethe and Ibsen? Were they overburdened by their own age? Their world was too much with them; and so they did not reach the highest peaks of tragedy: they were not universal.

96

What is Modern

It is time we erected a standard whereby to test what is modern. To be an adherent of all the latest movements—that is at most to be anarchistic, eclectic, inconsistent—call it what you will. Futurism, Realism, Feminism, Traditionalism may be all of them opposed or irrelevant to modernity. It is not sufficient that movements should be new—if they are ever new; the question is, To what end are they? If they are movements in the direction of emancipation, "the elevation of the type Man," then they are modern; if they are not, then they are movements to be opposed or ignored by moderns. If modernism be a vital thing it must needs have roots in the past and be an essential expression of humanity, to be traced, therefore, in the history of humanity: in short, it can only be a tradition. The true modern is a continuator of tradition as much as the Christian or the conservative: the tine fight between progress and stagnation is always a fight between antagonistic *traditions*. To battle against tradition *as such* is, therefore, not the task of the modern; but rather to enter the conflict—an eternal one—for his tradition against its opposite: Nietzsche found for this antithesis the symbolism of Dionysus and Apollo. Does such a tradition of modernity exist? Is there a "modern spirit" not dependent upon time and place, and in all ages modern? If there is—and there is—the possession of it in some measure will alone entitle us to the name of moderns, give us dignity and make the history of Man once more dramatic and tragical. It is a pity that some historian has not yet traced, in its expression in events, the history of this conflict—a task requiring the deepest subtlety and insight. Meantime, for this tradition may be claimed with confidence such events as Greek Tragedy, most of the Renaissance, and the emancipators of last century. These are triumphant expressions of "the modern spirit," but that spirit is chiefly to be recognized as a principle not always triumphant or easy of perception, constantly struggling, assuming many disguises and tirelessly creative. It is not, indeed, only a tradition of persons, of dogmas, or of sentiments: it is a principle of Life itself. This conception, it is true, is grand, and even terrifying—a disadvantage in this age. But is there any other which grants modernity more than the status of an accident of time and fashion?

97

How We Shall Be Known

In an age it is not always what is most characteristic that survives: posterity will probably know us not by our true qualities, but by the exceptions to them. The present-day writers in English who will endure after their age has passed are probably Joseph Conrad, W. H. Hudson, and Hillaire Belloc for a few of his essays and lyrics—none of them representative, none of them modern. They might have been born in any era: they are in the oldest tradition. The most striking characteristic of our time, however, is its lack of a tradition. The sentiment of transiency is our most deeply rooted sentiment: it is the very spirit of the age. But by its essential nature it cannot hope to endure, to be known by future generations; for we shall not produce immortal works until we become interested in some idea long enough to be inspired by it, and to write monumentally and surely of it. We hold our ideas by the day; but for a masterpiece to be born, an idea must have taken root and defied time. Permanence of form, moreover, would seriously embarrass a modern writer, who wishes to change with the hour, and does not want his crotchets of yesterday to live to be refutations of his fads of today. Thus we are too fleeting to make even our transitoriness eternal. The very sentiment of immortality has perished amongst us, and we actually prefer that our work should die—witness the Futurists! The most self-conscious heirs of modernity, these propounded the theory that *it is better* that works of art should not endure: well, in that case, their own creations have been true works of art! Nevertheless, all they did in this theory was to erect into a system the shallowness, provinciality and frivolousness of the present—and thereby to proclaim themselves the enemies of the future.

IV
ART AND LITERATURE

98

Psychology of Style

There are writers with a style—it may be either good or bad—and writers with no style at all, who just write badly. What quality or combination of qualities is it which makes a writer a stylist?

Style probably arises out of a duality; the association in a writer of the scribe and the spectator. The first having set down his thought, the second goes aside, contemplates it, as things should be contemplated, *from a distance*, and and asks, "How does this strike me? How does it look, sound, move?" And he suggests here a toning down of colour, there an acceleration of speed, somewhere else, it may be, an added lucidity, for clearness is an æsthetic as well as an intellectual virtue.

The writer without style, however, just writes on without second thought; the spectator is altogether lacking in him; he cannot contemplate his work from a distance, nor, indeed, at all. This explains the unconsciousness and innocence in bad writing—not in bad style, which is neither unconscious nor innocent! The stylist, on the other hand, is always the actor to his own spectator; he must get his effect; even Truth he uses as a means to his effect. If a truth is too repulsive, he throws this or that cloak over it; if it is uninteresting, he envelops it in mysticism (mysticism is simply an artist's trick); in a word, he æstheticizes, that is, falsifies everything, to please the second person in his duality, the spectator. Even if he gets his effects by moderation of statements, he is to be distrusted, for it is the moderation and not Truth that is aimed at. And, then, his temptation to employ metaphors, to work up an interesting madness, to rhapsodize—these most potent means to great effects, these falsifications! Well, are we to assent, then, to the old philosophic prejudice against style and refuse to believe any philosopher who does not write badly?

99

Modern Writing

The greatest fault of modern style is that it is a smirking style. It fawns upon the reader, it insinuates, it has the manner of an amiable dog. If it does something smart, it stops immediately, wags its tail, and waits confidently for your approval. You will guess now why those little regiments of dots are scattered so liberally over the pages of the best-known English novelist. It is H.G. Wells's style wagging its tail.

100

The Precise

There have been writers—there *are* writers—whose only title to fame is an interesting defect. They are unable to write soundly, and this inability, being abnormal, is more interesting than sound writing, which is only normal. For to limp or to hop on one leg is never pedestrian—what do I say?—is *not even* pedestrian.

101

Paradox

What is paradox? The "bull" raised to a form of literary art?

102

The Platitude

There should be no platitudes in the works of a sincere author. A platitude is an idea not understood by its writer—in one word, a shibboleth.

103

Praise?

It is usual to extol the industry of those realists who put *everything* into their books, but they should rather be censured for their want of taste. The truth is that they lack the selective faculty—lack, that is, art. Afraid to omit anything from their reproductions of existence—lest they omit what is most significant—they include *all*: the easiest course. The easiest course, that is—for the writers.

104

Hostility of Thinkers

When a thinker has a world of thought of his own, he generally becomes cold towards other thinkers, and to none more than to him whose star is nearest his own. It is necessary, therefore, that he should read, above all, the philosopher whose thought most closely resembles his, for to him he is most likely to be unjust. We are the most hostile to those who say what we say, but say it in a way we do not like.

105

The Twice Subtle

The thinker who has been twice subtle arrives at simplicity. And in doing so he has, at the same time, discovered a new truth. But this other thinker has possessed simplicity from the beginning. Has he also possessed this truth? At any rate, he does not know it.

106

Mastery of One's Thoughts

One should know how to keep one's thoughts at a distance. The French can do this, and, therefore, write at once wittily and profoundly of serious things. But the Germans live, perhaps, too near their thoughts, and are possessed by them: hence, their obscurity and heaviness. Wit—lightness of hand—shows that one is master of one's thought, and is not mastered by it. Nevertheless, the thoughts of the Germans may be the mightier. In this matter the complete thinker should be able to become French or German as occasion demands.

107

Psychologists

The keenest psychologists are those who are burdened with no social mission and get along with a minimum of theory. Joseph Conrad, for instance, is infinitely more subtle in his analysis of the human mind and heart than is H. G. Wells or John Galsworthy. He has the happy unconcern and detachment of a connoisseur in humanity, of one who experiences the same fine interest in an unusual human situation as the dilettante finds in some recondite trifle. Henry James carried this attitude to a high degree of refinement. He walked among men and women as a botanist might walk among a collection of "specimens," dismissing the ordinary with the assured glance of an expert, and lingering only before the distinctive and the significant. Should we who nurse a mission deplore the spirit in which these disinterested observers enter into their task? By no means. But for them, certain domains of human nature would never have been discovered, and we should have been correspondingly the losers. For we revolutionists must know the human kind before we can alter them. The non-missionary is as necessary as the missionary, and to none more than to the missionary.

108

Realism

Novels which take for their subject-matter mere ordinary, pedestrian existence—and of this kind are three-fourths of present-day novels—are invariably dull in one of two ways. In the first instance, they are written by pettifogging talents to whom only the ordinary is of interest, by people, that is to say, who are incapable of writing a book that is not dull. In the other, they are written by men generally of considerable, sometimes of brilliant, ability, who, misled by a theory, concern themselves laboriously with a domain of life which they dislike and which even bores them. But if the writer is bored, how much more so must be the reader! In short, the realist theory produces bad books because it forces the writer to select subjects the only emotion towards which it is possible to feel is boredom. And great art may arise out of hate, grief, even despair, but never out of boredom.

109

Fate and Mr. Wells

Fate has dealt ironically with H. G. Wells. It has turned his volumes of fiction into prophecies, and his volumes of prophecies into fiction.

110

Mr. G. K. Chesterton

A man's philosophy may be uninteresting, although he writes about it in an interesting manner. Just as the many write dully about interesting things, so a few write interestingly about dull things. And Mr. Chesterton is one of these. Equality is a dull creed, Christianity is a dry bone, tradition is wisdom for ants and the Chinese. But Mr. Chesterton is a very interesting man. How is it possible for an interesting man to have an uninteresting philosophy? Is this simply the last paradox of a master of paradox?

Mr. Chesterton's most charming quality is a, capacity for being surprised. He writes paradoxically, because to him everything is a paradox—the most simple thing, the most uninteresting thing. And that is his weakness, as well as his strength. He has found the common things so wonderful that he has not searched for the uncommon things. The average man is to him such a miracle, that he will not admit the genius is a far greater miracle. The theories he finds established, Christianity, equality, democracy, traditionalism, interest him so much that he has not gone beyond them to inquire into other theories perhaps more interesting. And this, because he lacks intellectual curiosity, along with that which frequently accompanies it, subtlety of mind. For the intellectually curious man is precisely the man who is *not* interested in things, or, at any rate, is interested in them only for a little, and then passes on or burrows deeper to find something further. One dogma after another he studies and deserts, this faith— less searcher, this philanderer, this philosopher; and that which leads him on is the hope that at last he will find something to interest him for an eternity. Perhaps it is this dissatisfaction of the mind which has always driven men to seek knowledge; perhaps, if all mankind had been like Mr. Chesterton, we should not have had even Christianity, equality, democracy and the other theories which he holds and adorns.

For Mr. Chesterton's impressions are all first impressions. Like his own deity, he sees everything for the first time always. And he lacks, therefore, the power, called vision, of seeing *into* things: the outside of things is already sufficiently interesting to him. He possesses imagination, however, and kindly and grotesque fancies which he hangs on the ear of the most common clodhopper of a reality. In fantasy he reaches greatness. But his philosophy is not interesting. It is himself that is interesting.

111

Nietzsche

Nietzsche loved Man, but not men: in that love were comprehended his nobility and his cruelty. He demanded that men should become Man before they asked to be loved.

112

Strindberg

This writer, despite his genius, earnestness and courage, arouses in us a feeling of profound disappointment. Nor is the cause very far to seek. For along with earnestness and courage in a writer we instinctively look for nobility and joy: if the latter qualities are absent we feel that the *raison d'être* of the former is gone, and that earnestness and courage divorced from nobility and joy are aimless, wasted, almost inconceivable. And in Strindberg they are so divorced. A disappointed courage; an ignoble earnestness! These are his pre-eminent qualities. And with them he essayed tragedy—the form of art in which nobility and joy are most required! As a consequence, the problems which he treats are not only treated inadequately; the inadequacy, when we stop to reflect upon it, absolutely amazes us. His crises are simply rows. His women, when they are angry, are intellectual fishwives; and—more disgusting still—so are his men. All his characters, indeed, intellectual and talented as they are, move on an amazingly low spiritual plane. The worst in their nature comes to light at the touch of tragedy, and an air of sordidness surrounds all. Posterity will not tolerate this "low" tragedy, this tragedy without a *raison d'être*, this drama of the dregs.

113

Dostoieffsky

Dostoieffsky depicted the subconscious as conscious; that was how he achieved his complex and great effects. For the subconscious is the sphere of all that is most primeval, mysterious and sublime in man; the very bed out of which springs the flower of tragedy. But did Dostoieffsky do well to lay bare that world previously so reverently hidden, and to bring the reader behind the scenes of tragedy? The artist will deny it—the artist who always demands as an ingredient in his highest effects mystery. For how can mystery be retained when the very realm of mystery, the subconscious, is surveyed and mapped? In Dostoieffsky's imperishable works the spirit of full tragedy is perhaps never evoked. What he provides in them, however, is such a criticism of tragedy as is nowhere else to be found. His genius was for criticism; the artist in him created these great figures in order that afterwards the psychologist might dissect them. And so well are they dissected, even down to the subconsciousness, that, to use a phrase of the critics, we know them better than the people we meet. Well, that is precisely what we object to—as lovers of art!

114

Again

Not only is Dostoieffsky himself a great psychologist; all his chief characters are great psychologists as well. Raskolnikoff, for instance, Porphyrius Petrovitch, Svidragaïloff, Prince Muishkin, walk through his pages as highly self-conscious figures, and as people who have one and all looked deeply into the shadowy world of human motives, and have generalized. The crises in Dostoieffsky's books are, therefore, of a peculiarly complex kind. It is not only the human passions and desires that meet one another in a conflict more or less spontaneous; the whole wealth of psychological observation and generalization of the conflicting character is thrown into their armoury, and with that, too, they do battle. The resulting effect is more large, rich and subtle than anything else in modern fiction, but also, if the truth must be told, more impure, in the artistic sense, more sophisticated. Sometimes, so inextricably are passion and "psychology" mingled, that the crises are more like the duels of psychologists than the conflicts of human souls. In the end, one turns with relief to the pure tragedy of the classical writers, the tragedy which is not brought about by people who act like amateur psychologists.

115

Tolerance of Artists

No matter what their conscious theories may be, all artists are unconsciously aristocratic, and even intolerant in their attitude to other men. They are more blind than most people to the *raison d'être* of the politician, the business man and the philosopher—these unaccountable beings who will not acknowledge the primacy of Creation and Beauty. But at last they magnanimously conclude that these exist to form their audience, *not* the subject-matter of their art—that is the modern fallacy!

116

Climate

There are natures exquisitely sensitive to their human environment. This man depresses them, they feel the vitality ebbing out of them in his presence; that other brings exhilaration, at the touch of his mind their powers increase and become creative. It is a question of atmosphere. The first has a wintry, grey soul; the latter carries a sun—*their* sun—in his bosom. And these artists require sunlight and soft air, before the flowers and fruit can hang from their boughs. Every artist of this type should go to Italy or France and live there; or, failing that, create for himself an Italy or France of friends. Others require the tempest with its lowering skies. But that is easier to seek; they can generally find it within themselves.

117

Sensibility

It may be wisdom for the man of action to smother his griefs, and follow resolutely his course. But with the artist it is different. He should not close his heart against sorrow, for sorrow is of use to him; his task is to transfigure it; thus he makes himself richer. Every conquest of suffering which is attained by isolating the pang makes the artist poorer; the part of him so isolated dies: he loses bit by bit his sensitiveness, and how much does his sensitiveness mean to him! The artist is more defenceless than other men, and he must be so. For his sensitiveness should be such that the faintest rose-leaf of emotion or thought cannot touch his heart without evoking in him infinite delight or pain; and, at the same time, he should be able to respond to the great tempests and terrible moods of life. Great strength, great love, great productiveness, these are required if he is to endure his sensitiveness; alas, for him, if he have them not! Then he must suffer and suffer, until he has cut off one by one the sources of his suffering, until he has mutilated and lamed what is most godlike in him, and has made himself ordinary at last—or a Schopenhauerian.

118

The Artist's Enemy

I waited once beside a lake, created surely to mirror Innocence, so pure it was. The passage of a butterfly over it or the breath of a rose-leaf's fall was enough to stir its surface, infinitely delicate and sensitive. Yet tempests did not affright it, for it laughed and danced beneath the whip of the fiercest storm. And it could bury, as in a bottomless tomb, the stones thrown at it by the most spiteful hands; to these, indeed, it responded with a Puck-like radiating smile that spread until it broke in soft laughter upon its marge. So strong and delicate it lay, and yet, it seemed, so defenceless. Yet what could harm it? Storm, shower, sunshine, and darkness alike but ministered to it, and even the missiles of its enemies were lost in its boundless security. It seemed invulnerable. I returned years later, and looked once, looked and fled. For the lake had grown old, blind and torpid, so that even the light lay dead in it. Then I noticed that on every side, almost invisible, there were innumerable black streams oozing—infection! The tragedy of the artist.

119

Uniformity

In the mien of children there is sometimes to be noted a natural nobility and pride; they walk with the unconscious grace of conquerors. But this grace and freedom soon disappear, and when the child has become man there is nothing left of them: his bearing is as undistinguished as his neighbour's. Nowhere, now, is nobility of presence and movement to be found, except among children, the chieftains of half-barbarous peoples, and some animals. The farther man departs from the animal the less dignified he becomes, and the more his appearance conforms to a common level: indeed, civilization seems, on one side, to be a labourious attempt to arrive at the undistinguished and indistinguishable. Is Man, then, the mediocre animal par excellence? Only, perhaps, under an egalitarian régime. Wherever a hierarchy exists in Europe there is more of nobility of demeanour than elsewhere. Equality and humility are the great fosterers of the mediocre: and not only, alas! of the mediocre in demeanour. Who can tell how many proud, graceful and gallant thoughts and emotions have been killed by shame— the shame which the egalitarians and the humble have heaped upon them? And how much Art, therefore, has lost? Certainly, in the minds of children there are many brave, generous and noble thoughts which are never permitted to come to maturity. Ye must become as little children——.

120

Immortality of the Artist

An artist one day forgot Death, so entirely had he become Life's, rapt in a world of living contemplation; and, established there, he created a form. That hour was immortal, and, therefore, the form was immortal. This is the "timelessness" of true art-work; they are fashioned "in eternity," as Blake said, and so speak to the eternal in Man.

121

The Descent of the Artist

At the beginning of his journey he climbed daringly, leaping from rock to rock, exuberant, tireless, until he reached what he thought was his highest peak. Then began his descent, and, lo, immediately great weariness fell upon him. A friend of his wondered, Is he going downhill because he is tired? Or is he tired because he is going downhill?

122

Apropos the Cynic

He wrote with an assumption of extreme heartlessness, and the public said, "How tender his heart must be when he hides it under *such* a disguise!" But what he was hiding all the time was his lack of heart.

123

Artist and Philosopher

In all ages the philosophers have *pardoned* the artists their lack of depth, on account of their divine love of the beautiful. In our time, however, this only reason for pardoning them has disappeared, and they are now entirely deserving of condemnation. For the realists abjure equally thought—interpretation, and beauty—selection. To be an eye, with a fountain pen attached to it; that is their aim, successfully attained, alas! A single eye and not a single thought: the definition of the realist.

124

An Evil

Art is at the present day far too easy for comprehension, far too obvious. Our immediate task should be to make it *difficult*, and the concern of a dedicated few. Thus only shall we win back reverence for it. When it is reverenced, however, it will then be time to extend its sway; but not until then. Art must be approached with reverence, or not at all. A democratic familiarity with it—such as exists among the middle classes, *not* among the working classes, in whom reverence is not yet dead—is an abomination.

125

Modern Art Themes

How sordid are the themes which modern art has chosen for itself! The loss of money or of position, poverty, social entanglements—the little accidents which a thinker laughs at! Are modern artists as bourgeois as this? A coterie of shop-keepers? Tragic art has no concern with the accidental: that is the sphere of comedy. Tragedy should move inevitably once it has begun to revolve; it is beyond fashion, universal, essential; Fate, not Circumstance, is its theme. The presence of the accidental in a tragedy is sufficient to condemn it. For it is the inevitable, the "Fate" in Tragedy, that makes of it a heroic and *joyful* thing. It cannot be improvised like Comedy. It demands in its creator a sense of the eternal, just as Comedy, on the other hand, demands an exquisite appreciation of temporal fashion. Tragedy is the greater art; Comedy, perhaps, the more difficult. Our modern tragedies, however, are mainly about accidents, and very mean accidents; they are improvised misfortunes and their effect is depressing.

126

The Illusionists

How shallow are most artists! How childish! How subject to illusion! This novelist at the end of his novels leaves his characters in a Utopia, from which all sorrow and trial have been banished, a condition absolutely unreal, contemptible and absurd. And all his readers admire without thinking, and call the author profound! He is not profound, but shallow and commonplace. Except for his gift of mimicry, which he calls Art, he is just an average man. And, moreover, he is tired: the "happy ending" is his exhaustion speaking through his art, his will to stagnation and surrender. Works of art should only end tragically, or enigmatically, as in "A Doll's House," or at the gateway of a new ideal, as in "An Enemy of the People."

127

Majorities and Art

When it is said that in modern society poetic tragedy is out of season and cannot *succeed*, an assumption is made which on literary grounds can never be admitted. It is that majorities count in literature as in politics; that "Brand" was a failure and "A Doll's House" a success. But from another point of view, "Brand" was the success, "A Doll's House" the failure. And the whole "problem" drama a failure with it, and all the realistic schools, as well—a failure! This is *certainly* how the future historian of literature will regard it. Our era with its depressing "masterpieces" will be called the barren era, because the grand *exception*, great art, has not bloomed in it, because even our critics have judged contemporary art by a criterion of success instead of the eternal spiritual criterion: their championship of "problem" art proves it! In the meantime, then, realism is considered "the thing," and people speak pityingly of poetic tragedy. Only those forms of art which can "survive" in the struggle for existence are counted good—so deeply, so unwisely have we drunk at the Darwinian spring!

128

The Decay of Man

The aim of Art was once to enrich existence by the creation of gods and demi-gods; it is now to duplicate existence by the portrayal of men. Art has become imitation, Realism has triumphed. And how much has materialism had to do with this! In an age lacking a vivid ideal of Man, men become interesting. The eyes of the artist, no longer having an ideal to feed upon, are turned towards the actual, and imitation succeeds creation. Every one busies himself in the study of men, and Art becomes half a science, the artists actually collecting their data, as if they were professors of psychology! Theories glorifying men are born, and the cult of the average man arises, which is nothing but the exaltation of men at the expense of Man. In due time all ideals perish, only an inspiration towards averageness remains, and equality is everywhere enthroned. Art has no longer a heaven to fly to, there to create loftier heavens. In despair, she descends to earth and the ordinary, and for her salvation *must* find the ordinary interesting, must *make* the ordinary interesting. Realism arises when ideals of Man decay: it is the egalitarianism of Art.

129

A New Valuation

But why do ideals of Man decay—why *did* the ideal of Man decay? Because there were no longer examples to inspire the artists in the creation of their grand, superhuman figures. Suspicion, envy, equality—call it what you will—had become strong: the great man could no longer fight it and remain great. By the radicals the genius was regarded as an insult to the remainder of mankind. And how ordinary he was, this genius, compared with the grand figures of the time of the Renaissance; that time when men were weighed and valued, when elevation and inequality were acknowledged and acted upon, and Man became greater in stature, with Art his Will to Greatness! Well, we must weigh men again; we must deny equality; we must affirm aristocracy—in everything but commerce and production, where democracy is really a return to the aristocratic tradition. And, you artists, you must turn from men to Man, from Realism to Myth. And if you can find in your age no example to inspire you to the creation of a great ideal of Man, then become your own examples! Man must be born again, if you would enter into your heaven.

130

The Man and the Hour

A. Let people say about aristocracy what they will, it remains true that Man generally is equal to the event. Events are the true stepping-stones on which Man rises to higher things. B. Ah! you are not speaking of Man, but of men, of the many. The great man, however, does not require an event to call his greatness forth. He is his own event—and also that of others!

131

The Lover to the Artists

Love idealizes the object. If you would create an ideal Art, must you not, then, learn to love? And that you are Realists—does it not prove that you have not Love?

132

Origin of the Tragic

Here is yet another guess at the origin of the tragic:

A man is told of some calamity, altogether unexpected, the engulfing of a vessel by the sea, an avalanche which wipes out a town, or a fire in which a family of little ones perish, leaving the father and mother unharmed and disconsolate; and at once the very grandest feelings awaken within him, he finds himself enlarged spiritually, and life itself is enriched for him— the people in the vessel and in the town, the children and the parents of the children, are raised to a little more than human elevation by the favouritism of calamity. Next day he hears that the news was false, and immediately, along with the feeling of relief, he experiences an unmistakable disappointment and loss; for all those grand emotions and the contemplation of life in that greater aspect are snatched from him! Perhaps in primitive times, when the means of disseminating news were more untrustworthy than they are today, disappointments of this kind would occur very often; and one day some rude poet, having noted the elevation which calamity brings, would in luxurious imagination *invent* a calamity, in order to experience *at will* this enlargement of the soul. But a tale of calamity, being invented, would inevitably please the poet's hearers, both for the feelings it aroused and the grand image of Man it represented. So much for the origin and persistence—not the meaning—of the tragic.

133

Tragedy and Comedy

Tragedy is the aristocratic form of art. In it the stature of Man is made larger. The great tragic figures are superhuman, unapproachable: we do not sorrow with them, but for them, with an impersonal pity and admiration. And that is because Man, and not men, is represented by them: idealization and myth are, therefore, proper to their delineation.

But Comedy is democratic. Its subject is men, the human-all-too-human, the unrepresentative: it belittles men in a jolly egalitarianism. This static fraternity, this acceptance of men as they are, is resented by the aristocratic natures, who would make Man nobler; but to the average men it is flattering, for it proclaims that the great are absurd even as they, it unites men in a brotherhood of absurdity. Thus, all comedy is an involuntary satire, all tragedy an involuntary idealization of men.

Tragedy is the supreme affirmation of Life, for it affirms Life even in its most painful aspects, struggle, suffering, death; so that we say, "Yes, this, too, is beautiful!" *That* was the *raison d'être* of classical tragedy—and not Nihilism!

Well, in which of these forms, Tragedy or Comedy, may our hopes and visions of the Future best be expressed? Surely in that which idealizes Man and says Yea to suffering, Tragedy, the dynamic form of Art.

134

Super-Art

In the works of some artists everything is on a slightly superhuman scale. The figures they create fill us with astonishment; we cannot understand how such unparalleled creatures came into being. When we contemplate them, in the works of Michelangelo or of Nietzsche, there arise unvoluntarily in our souls sublime dreams of what Man may yet attain. Our thoughts travel into the immeasurable, the undiscovered, and the future becomes almost an intoxication to us.

In Nietzsche, especially, this attempt to make Art perform the impossible—this *successful* attempt to make Art perform the impossible—is to be noted in every book, almost in every word. For he strains language to the utmost it can endure; his words seem to be striving to escape from the bonds of language, seeking to transcend language. "It is my ambition," he says in "The Twilight of the Idols," "to say in ten sentences what every one else says in a whole book—what every one else does *not* say in a whole book." In the same way, when in his first book he wrote about Tragedy, he raised it to an elevation greater than it had ever known before, except, perhaps, in the works of Æschylus; when, in his essay upon "Schopenhauer as Educator," he adumbrated his conception of the philosopher, philosophy seemed to become a task for the understandings of gods; and when, having criticized the prevailing morality, he set up another, it seemed to his generation an impossible code for human beings, a code cruel, over-noble. Finally, when he wrote of Man, it was to create the Superman. He touched nothing which he did not ennoble. And, consequently, in Art his chosen form was Myth; he held it beneath the nobility of great art to create anything less than demi-gods; religion and art were in him a unity.

In super-art, in these works of Leonardo and Michelangelo, of Æschylus and Nietzsche, Man is incited again and again to surpass himself, to become more than "human."

135

Love Poetry

Love poetry, so long as it glorifies Love, is supremely worthy of our reverence. Everything that idealizes and transfigures Love, making it more desirable and full even of transcendental meaning, is of unquestionable advantage to mankind; on the other hand, a crudely physiological statement, even though this may be *formally* true, serves neither Love nor Life. It is assuredly not the function of art to treat Love in this way. On the contrary, amatory poetry by its idealization allures to Love; this is true even of such of it as is tragic: we are prepared by it to experience gladly even the suffering of Love. The only poetry that is noxious is that which bewails the "vanity" of Love, and that in which a deliberate sterility is adumbrated. These are decadent.

136

Literature and Literature

Literature that is judged by literary standards merely is not of the highest rank. For the greatest works are themselves the standards by which literature is judged. How, then, are they to be valued? By a standard outside of literature, by their consonance with that which is the *raison d'être* of literature? In them a far greater problem than any literary problem faces us, the problem, Why does literature exist? What is the meaning of literature?

Through whole generations men forget this problem, and literature becomes to them a specialized form of activity to be pursued for its own sake, a part of Man's soul, thrown off and become static and separate, with a sterile life of its own. The more shallow theory and practice of literature then come into being; Realism and Art for Art's sake flourish. But the eternal question always returns again, Why does literature exist? What is its meaning? And, then, the possibility of another blossoming of literature is not far away.

137

The Old Poet

An old poet who had lived in the good days when poets were *makers*—of moralities and gods, among other things—lately re-visited the earth, and after a study of the very excellent exercises in literature to be found in our libraries, delivered himself thus:—

"How has our power decayed! Into litterateurs have we declined who were creators. Perish all literature that is only literature! Poets live to create gods; to glorify gods should all their arts of adornment and idealization be used. But I see here adornment without the object worthy of adornment; beautification for the sake of beautification; Art for Art's sake. These artists are only half artists. They have surely made Art into a game."

The critics did not understand him, and, *therefore,* disagreed. The artists thought he was mad, besides knowing nothing of æsthetics. The moral fanatics acclaimed him vociferously, mistaking him for a popular preacher. Only a philosophico-artistic dilettante listened attentively, and said, a little patronizingly, "He is wrong, but he is more right than wrong."

138

The Old Gods

Perhaps there is too much made of anthropomorphism. Man's first gods were not "human" gods; they were stars, animals, plants and the like. It was not until he became an artist that he made gods after his own form: anthropomorphism is just an artistic convention! For gods are in their *content* superhuman. There has never been a man like Jehovah or Zeus or Odin. The essential thing in them is that they embody an ideal, a fiction, adumbrating something *more* than Man. Religion is poetry in the grand style, and, as poetry, must have its conventions.

139

The Old Poets

In primitive times the poet was far more both of an inventor and a liar than he is at present. For many centuries the lies of the poets have been innocent lies, a convention merely, and to be recognized as such before "æsthetic" enjoyment can begin. But the lies the old poets told were believed literally—as they were meant to be! Yes, the poet at the beginning was just a liar, a great liar. How else, if he had not deceived Man, could he have peopled the heavens with Man's deities? And as the father of whole families of gods, he has done more to decide the fate of Humanity than all the philosophers, heroes and martyrs. These are only his servants, who explain war or die for his fictions. And not merely error, as Nietzsche held, but lying has from the earliest times been the most potent factor of progress. But not all lying; only the lies told out of great love have been creative and life-giving. Art, imagination, prophecy, hallucination, ecstasy, vision—all these were united in the first poets, the true creators.

140

The Creator Redivivus

The only modern who has dared to be a poet through and through, that is, a liar in the noble and tragic sense, is the author of the Superman. In Nietzsche, again, after centuries of divine toying, the poet has appeared in his great *rôle* of a creator of gods, a figure beside whom the "poet" seems like nothing more than the page boy of the Muse.

141

Literature as Praise

A. Would you erase from the book of literature all that is not idealization and myth, you neo-moderns? Would you deprive us of all the charming, serious, whimsical, and divinely frivolous works which are human-all-too-human? B. If we could—a thousand times no! We would only destroy what defames Life. All that praises Life, all that enchants to Life, we would cherish as things holy. Idealization, it is true, is the highest form of praise, because it arises out of Love; but there are other forms. Modern Realism, however, is a calumny against Life. *Écrasez l'infâme!*

142

The Poet Speaks

How unhappy must all those poor mortals be who are not poets! They feel and cannot express. They are dumb when their soul would utter its divinest thoughts. Cloddish and fragmentary, they are scarcely human, these poor mortals! For one must be a poet to be altogether human. Yes! in the ideal society of the future every one will be a poet, even the average man!

143

Myth

The worst evil of our time is this, that there is nothing greater than the current average existence to which man can look; Religion has dried up, Art has decayed from an idealization of life into a reflection of it. In short, Art has become a passive thing, where once it was the "great stimulus to Life." The idealization and enchantment which the moderns have so carefully eliminated from it was precisely its *raison d'être*. And modern Art, which sets out to copy life, has forgotten Art altogether, its origin, its meaning and its end.

Against this aimless Realism, we must oppose idealization, and especially that which is its highest expression, Myth. And let no one say that it is impossible at this stage in Man's history to resuscitate Myth. The past has certainly lost its mystery for us, and it was in the past, at the source of Humanity, that the old poets set their sublime fictions. But the future is still ours, and there, at Man's goal, our myths must be planted. And thither, indeed, has set the great literature of the last hundred years. Faust, Mephistopheles, Brand, Peer Gynt, Zarathustra—there were no greater figures in the literature of the last century—were all myths, and all forecasts of the future. The soil out of which literature grows, then, has not yet been exhausted! If we but break away from Realism, if we make Art symbolic, if we bring about a marriage between Art and Religion, Art will rise again. That this is possible, we who have faith in the Future *must* believe.

V
CREATIVE LOVE

144

Creative Love

To us who nourish hopes for the future of Man, the important distinction to be drawn in Love is not that between the sacred and the profane. We ask, rather, Is our Love creative or barren? That Love should bring happiness, or union, or fulfilment, seems to us not such a very great matter! The will to create something, out of oneself, not oneself, whether it be in bodies, or in Art or Philosophy—that is the thing for ever worthy of our reverence.

There is another Love; that whose end is enjoyment. It is the enemy of creative Love. It is the Love which, in various forms, is known as Liberalism, or Humanitarianism, or the greatest happiness of the greatest number. Sympathy is its central dogma; and it is never tired of exalting itself at the expense of the other Love, which it calls cruel, senseless and unholy. But the same blasphemy is here repeated that Socrates once was guilty of and afterwards so divinely atoned. For it is not creative Love, but sympathetic Love, that is unholy. This would spare the beloved the pangs of love, even if, in doing so, it had to sacrifice the fruits of love. It springs from disbelief in existence. Life is suffering, it cries, suffering must be alleviated, and, therefore, Life must be abated, weakened and lamed! And this love is barren. But creative Love does not bring enjoyment, but rapture and pain. It is the will to suffer gladly; it finds relief from the pains of existence, not in alleviation, but in creation. This Love is, indeed, a Siren—we would not mitigate the awfulness of that symbol—luring Man to peril, perhaps to shipwreck. Yet, by the holiest law of his being, he listens, he follows. And, if his ears have been sealed by reason he *unseals* them again, he listens with his very soul, yielding to that which is for him certainly danger, perhaps Death, knowing that, even in Death, he will be affirming Life in the highest. This Love, the earnest of future greatness, this terrible, unconditional and innocent thing, we *cannot but* reverence.

145

Where Man is Innocent

There is one region in Man where innocence and a good conscience still reign—in the unconscious. Love and the joy in Love are of the unconscious. The rapture which Love brings is neither, as Schopenhauer said, merely a device to ensure the propagation of mankind, nor the race rejoicing in and through the individual to its own perpetuation; but the joy of unconscious Man, still innocent as before the Fall, with a good conscience enjoying the anticipatory rapture of new life. The instincts believe in Life entirely without questioning; doubt and guilt are simply not present in their world: it is reflection that makes sinners of us all.

The thoughts that come to us in the season of Love—we do not need to search in metaphysical heavens for their source. They arise from the very well spring, the very central ego of Man, out of the unconscious, the innocent, the real. Poetry, in that which is incomprehensible and mystical in it, arises from this also. So there is hope still for Man, all ye who believe not in primal depravity! The real man is *even now* innocent: Original Sin is only mind deep, conscience deep. The instincts still behave as if Life-defaming doctrines *were not*: they have not yet begun to mourn at the Spring and exult at the Autumn. And in the ecstasies of creative Love, whether it be of persons or of things, they continue to celebrate, without misgiving, their jubilee.

146

A Criterion

To find out whether a thing is decadent or no, let us henceforth put this question, Does it spring from creative Love? Is the Will to suffering incarnate in it, or the will to alleviate suffering? How much must by this standard be condemned! Humanitarianism and its child, Reform, or the desire to alleviate others' pain; Æstheticism and its step-brother, Realism, or the wish to alleviate one's own: these spring from the same source—a dearth of Love. For creative Love would enjoin, not sympathy with suffering, but the will to transcend suffering; not reform, whose aim is happiness, but revolution, whose aim is growth; not Art for Art's sake, an escape from Life into a stationary æsthetic world, but the creation, out of Life, of ever new Art; not Realism or the need to find men interesting; but idealization, or the desire to *make* men interesting. John Galsworthy and Oscar Wilde alike are decadent for this reason, that they lack Love. The real difference between them is that the one is a Collectivist, and sympathizes with the people, and the other is an Individualist, and sympathizes with himself. But both degrade Love to the level of Hedonism; both rebel against the cruelty of Love, desiring a Love which will not hurt, and, therefore, *must* be barren.

But wherever peoples, faiths or arts decay, the decay of Love—this strong, energetic Love—has come first. The current frivolousness about intellectual matters, the philandering of the literary coquettes, springs simply from a lack of Love. For the great problems demand passion for their comprehension, and our intellectuals dislike passion. In politics and in religion it is the same: creative Love has everywhere disappeared to be replaced by barren Sympathy. But is it possible by preaching to increase Love? Can it be willed into power? Well, praise may call it forth.

147

Love at the Renaissance

How may a great creative age like the Renaissance be interpreted on the hypothesis of Love? Shall it yet be found that the mainspring of the Renaissance was a newly discovered love of Life and, therefore, of Man?

In the Middle Ages that part of Life, then called God, had become isolated and abstract, and was worshipped to the detriment of all other Life; while Man was neglected where he was not belittled. Thus, a strong current of Man's love was diverted away from Man altogether, and the earth became dark and sterile. How was the earth to recapture its love again, and drink back into itself its rapture and creativeness? By a marriage in which God and the Universe were made one flesh; by the incorporation of God into Life, and, therefore, into Man. Hence arose the Pantheism of the Renaissance. To love Life with a good conscience, to love Life unconditionally, it was necessary to call Life God. Out of this Love sprang not only the art but the science of the Renaissance. For Man once more became interested in himself, and, from himself, in Life; ultimately discoveries were made and more than one New World was brought to light.

Perhaps it is the defect of all theistic, objective theologies that they become, sooner or later, barren. Only by being translated into the subjective do they regain their creative power: Pantheism is the remedy for Theism. Yet to Theism we owe this, that it lent intensity and elevation to Love. The Love of the Pantheists of the Renaissance was not ordinary human Love; it united in a unique emotion the love that had formerly been given to Man along with that which had formerly been given to God. It loved Man as God should be loved—a dangerous thing. But out of this love of God in Man it created, nevertheless, something great, somewhat less than the one, somewhat more than the other—the demi-god. The Renaissance was the age of the demi-gods.

148

Sympathy

Sympathy is Love bereft of his bow and arrows—but still blind.

149

A Self-Evident Proposition

This is certain, that God is Love. How, else, could He have created the Universe?

150

"God is Love"

When Jesus said, "God is Love," He denned a religion of Becoming. Was it not necessarily so? For Love is not something which may *choose* to create; it *must* create, it is fundamentally the will and the power to create. And Eternal Love, or God, is, therefore, eternal creation, eternal change, eternal Becoming. Consequently, there is no ultimate goal, no Perfection, except that which is realized at every moment in the self-expression of Love. A vision? A nightmare? Well, it depends whether one is in favour of Life, or of Death; whether one lives, or is lived. And, therefore, whether religion is subjective, or objective? Whether God is within us, or outside us? For so long as God is within us, we must create. That should be our Becoming!

151

Love and Mr. Galsworthy

The art of Mr. Galsworthy is such an ambiguous thing—half impersonal portrayal, half personal plea, the *Art pour l'Art* of a social reformer—and the subjects he chooses are so controversial—the abuses of society—that it is hard to place him as an artist. When "The Dark Flower" appeared, however, we thought we had him. Here was a great subject to his hand, an artist's question at last, Love. Alas! even in writing about it, he could not altogether exclude the reformer. Well, that itself, perhaps, told us something! However that may be, we do get here Mr. Galsworthy's conception of Love. It is an inadequate conception, a realist's conception: Love, with the meaning left out. The ardours, the longing, the disappointment and anguish—all the *symptoms*—of Love are given; but not a hint that Love has any significance beyond the emotions it brings: that which redeems Love, creation, is ignored altogether! Mr. Galsworthy has seen that Love is cruel, but he has not seen beyond the cruelty: it is the ultimate thing to him. Well, that is perhaps the most that could be expected of a humanitarian trying to comprehend Love! In this book are all the symptoms of Humanitarianism—pity for every one, reform of institutions, suffering always considered the sufficient reason for abolishing or palliating things: a creed thrice inadequate, thrice shallow, thrice blind. Love would find relief from suffering in creation. But one feels that Mr. Galsworthy would abolish Life if he could. Humanitarianism unconsciously seeks the annihilation of Life, for in Life suffering is integral.

152

Mr. Thomas Hardy

In Mr. Hardy's conception of Love, unlike Mr. Galsworthy's, the contingency of creation is never absent; but to him creation is not a justification of the pangs of Love. It is an intensification of them; it is Love's last and worst indignity. But even when Love does not bestow this ultimate insult of creation, it cannot resist the satisfaction of torturing its victims; it is wanton and irrelevant in its distribution of pain. Mr. Hardy's books are filled with the torments of Love. Was it not fitting that he should aim his main indictment of Life against it, seeing that it is the trick whereby the blunder of Life is perpetuated? And so Mr. Hardy is certainly a decadent; but he is a great decadent—one of those who by the power of their denial of Life seem to make Life more profound and tragic, and inspire the healthy artists to an even greater love and reverence for it.

He is great, however, not by his theories, but by his art. The contrast between the sordidness of his thought and the splendidness of his art fills us sometimes with amazement. He sets out in his books to prove that Life is a mean blunder; and, in spite of himself, the tragedy of this blunder becomes in his hands splendid and impressive, so that Life is enriched even while it is defamed. Art, which is *necessarily* idealization and glorification, triumphs in him over even his most deeply founded conscious ideas. In all his greater books, it refutes his pessimism and turns his curses into involuntary blessings. So divine is Art!

153

Mr. George Moore

In writing about Love, Mr. Moore falls into the same realistic error as Mr. Galsworthy: he writes about its manifestations without knowledge of that which gives them meaning and connection. Love to him is just certain sensations—and not only Love, but everything else. Art is a sensation; religion, a sensation; the soul, a sensation. Take out of his books sensation, and there will be little of account left. He knows the religious feeling, but not religion: he always confounds spirituality with refined sensualism. So he knows the sensation of Love, but not Love.

But Mr. Moore is learned in the senses: he knows them in everything but their purity. Yes, even sensuality is in his books corrupted. How true this is we realize when in "Evelyn Innes" he compares one of his characters to a faun. We are almost distressed at this, for we feel that the word is not only coarsened, but used with a wrong meaning altogether: we feel that Mr. Moore is incapable of understanding what a faun is! These sophisticated, scented and somewhat damaged voluptuaries of his, in whose conversation there is always an atmosphere of expensive feminine lingerie, and who "know" women so intimately; how perverted must be the taste which can compare them with the hardy, nimble, unconscious creatures of ancient Greece! But Mr. Moore is much nearer in temper to Oscar Wilde than to the realists. He is an æsthete essentially, and a realist only in the second place, and only because he is an æsthete. The province of selected exquisite beauty had been exhausted by Wilde and his school; so Mr. Moore turned to the squalid, the commonplace and the diseased in Life, there to find his "æsthetic emotion." This explains the curious effect at once of colour and of drabness in his books. He is a perverted Wilde; doubly a decadent.

Mr. Bernard Shaw

Both the strength and the weakness of Mr. Shaw spring from a defect—his lack of Love. Freedom from illusion is his strength. He possesses common sense minus common sentiment; that, and probably nothing more; and that gives to his thought an appearance of subtlety, though it is not really subtle. Thus, his common sense tells him that Love is essentially creation. He sees through the illusions which Love spins round its purpose, because he does not see these illusions at all. Love, indeed, is known to him in all but its illusions; but who knows Love that knows not Love's illusions? Still, it is to his honour that he has conceived Love as creation. His weakness consists in that his attitude to Love is purely intellectual. He lacks Love more than any other man of his time. In grappling with the great problems of existence, it is not Love but the very absence of Love that has been his most useful weapon; and so he has seen much, but grasped nothing, created nothing. And because he has never loved, he can never be called an artist. For how can one who has not loved idealize? And how can one who has not idealized be an artist? In Mr. Shaw, Nature has gone out of her way to create the very antithesis of the artist.

What Nietzsche said about Socrates is true of Mr. Shaw even in a higher degree; that his reason is stronger than his instincts, and has usurped the place of his instincts. Without Love, he yet affirms creation. What can be his reason for doing so? Why should he wish Life to persist if he does not love Life? Is it in order that people might still converse wittily, and the epigram might not die? Or so that exceptional men might experience forever the joy of intellectual conflict, the satisfaction found in the ruthless exposure of fallacy and weakness, and the proud feeling of mental power? We know that Mr. Shaw regards the brain as an end—the purpose of Life being to perfect a finer and finer brain—and we know, too, that to Mr. Shaw the highest joy the brain can experience is not that of knowing, but of fighting.

Knowledge to him is a weapon with which to wage war. Does he desire Life to continue so that controversy might continue? Well, let us look, then, for some other reason for his praise of Love. He himself lacks Love:—Can it be that he praises it for the same reason for which the Christian praises what he is not but would fain be? And his love of Love is then something pathetic, founded on "unselfishness"? And himself, a Romantic?

155

Mr. H. G. Wells

How much has Mr. Wells's scientific training had to do with his conception of Love? As a student of biology, it was natural he should see Love as sex. In all his theories, indeed, there is more of the scientist than of the artist. Scientific certainly, is his simple acceptance of sex as a fact, and his unhesitating association of it with generation, and of both with Love. The innocence of the scientist and not of the artist is his, an innocence Darwinian, not Goethean. And so, although his purpose is fine—to restore in his books an innocent conception of sexual Love—in doing so, his biology always runs away with his art. For he would render sex significant by reading it into all creation, as the meaning of creation; thus making the instrument more than the agent, the very meaning of the agent! But this robs both creation and sex of their significance. The way to restore an innocent conception of sexual Love is by reading creation into it, by seeing it as part of the universal Becoming, by carrying it away on the great purifying stream of Becoming. In spite of his genius, and still more of his cleverness, Mr. Wells here began at the wrong end. But it is doubtful whether any one in this generation has sufficient artistic power and elevation to express in art this conception of Love. Within the limits of Realism, especially of "physiological Realism," it certainly cannot be expressed. Nothing less than the symbolic may serve for it.

156

The Idealism of Love

The writer who discovered that love idealizes the object might have pushed his discovery a little further; for it is no less true that love idealizes the subject. None knows better than the poets how to take advantage of this self-idealization: one has only to read their love poems to find out how much more is said about the poet's beautiful feelings than about the object which presumably evoked them. Heine, particularly, was a shameless offender in this way. A woman was to him simply an excuse for seeing himself in imagination in a romantic attitude. But even with the others who appear less obtrusive and more disinterested the implication is the same. How elevated and even divine we must be, they seem to say, when we can feel in this manner; and how happy, when we are privileged to love an object of such loveliness! Yes! love has such power that it idealizes everything—even the subject!

157

Love and Becoming

The great Heraclitus propounded the doctrine of Becoming. Everything changes, is built up and dissolved; "stability" is only a little sluggishness in the flux of things. Zeus, the great child, the divine artist, constructs and destroys at his pleasure and for his amusement: all the worlds are his playthings. This conception of the Universe is innocent and beautiful, an artist's conception; but it is at the same time terrifying. And that because all meaning is left out of it; for all things without meaning, no matter how beautiful they may be, are in the end terrifying.

Nietzsche, the modern counterpart of Heraclitus, re-affirmed this doctrine; but he coupled with it the idea of creative Love: that is his chief distinction. Certainly, those who do not comprehend Nietzsche's Love do not comprehend Nietzsche. It is the key to his religion of Becoming. Becoming without Love is meaningless; Love without Becoming is meaningless. But, united, each gives its meaning to the other, each redeems the other. But have things a meaning in themselves? Is it not Man that forever interprets and interprets? Very well. But is not a thing incomplete without its interpretation? Is not its interpretation a part of it?

158

Static Values

Stagnant waters become noisome after a while. And stagnant values? Certainly within these eternal pools not a few repulsive things have been born: in Perfection, Sin; in Justice, Guilt. It was when human judgments were apotheosized and became Eternal Justice that guilt was insinuated into the core of Life. A falsehood, a presumption! What man found necessary at one moment in his history for his preservation, that, forsooth, was a law governing the spheres, the everlasting edict of God Himself. And when Life did not operate in conformity with this law, it was Life that must needs be guilty—a very ingenious method of world-vilification! It was human vanity that created the eternal verities. And how much have we suffered from them! For the deification of Things meant the diabolization of Man, nay, of Life itself. The metaphysician who created Heaven created Hell at the self-same moment; but, ever since, it has been Hell that has given birth to the metaphysicians. Being *condemns* Becoming, and pollutes all Life with sin. So in the pools of Being we can no longer cleanse ourselves, and our preference for a doctrine of Becoming may be at bottom a hygienic preference.

159

The God of Becoming

Love is the God of Becoming. All the other gods are static gods, changeless for yesterday, today and tomorrow. But Love belongs altogether to the future. It is the deity of those who would create a future.

160

Utopias

It is sympathy that has built the Utopias. On every one of them is written, "Conflict and suffering are bad." Utopia is nothing but a place where men are happy, like how many heavens, an ideal of exhaustion. The thing that is omitted from it is always Love, for Love would shatter all Utopias and leave them behind. In Nowhere Man no longer creates, but enjoys. But creation and pain go hand in hand; for what is creation? The dissolution of the outworn, the birth of the new; a continuous fury in which the throes of death and of life are mingled. And Love calls Man to that fate.

What we need is an ideal of energy. But that must needs be an ideal of Man, not of Society; for Man is the dynamic, Society the static. Utopia is a goal, but the Superman is a goal beyond a goal; for, once attained, he is naught but the arrow to shoot into *his* future. To attain the Superman is to surpass the Superman. Only ideals of this kind are unassailable by Love.

161

"Primacy of Things"

If we aim at a state of society in which static values, as far as we can know them, are conformed with, we aim at a state in which the creative impulse will not only be needless, but harmful. For does not belief in absolute values necessarily imply belief in a Utopia? And therefore in something antagonistic to Love? The metaphor of static Perfection, lovely as it is, has perhaps ruled us too long, and it is time we superseded it by another. Or is it still, as it has always been, a crime to substitute one metaphor for another? Even if it is Love that drives us on?

Progress conceived as a discovery of the unknown instead of as a pursuit of Perfection—might not that take us a long way? Did Nietzsche, perhaps, create his Superman, and give him his hardness and lightness for no other purpose than to carry out that task? Perfection is something that we have yet to discover! In this conception of progress all Utopias are transcended, all goals renounced, yet a set of values, a morality, is retained. The morality might be judged by the criterion, Does it aid us in our quest? A future of discovery, of creation and change, not of enjoyment: what a task for energetic Love does that open out! The Superman is a goal, but what is the Superman's goal? The Superman is something that must be surpassed!

162

Perfection

When men write largely of Perfection, as if it were a concept every one could understand, we are entitled to ask what exactly they mean. Do they mean a sort of synthesis or hotchpotch of the virtues in which they believe? Does X believe in a Christian and Y in a Nietzschean perfection? As a rule, conceptions of Perfection are offshoots of the morality prevalent at any given time. And, for action, people's conception of Perfection is much more important than Perfection itself. Therefore, let us ceaselessly repeat, Perfection is something still to be discovered! As for the current conception, is conflict an ingredient in it, or rest? Is it an ideal of Life, or a thing impossible, self-contradictory, static, an eternal stick with which to chastise existence? The first question to be asked.

163

Goals

When people speak of the unthinkableness of eternal Becoming which has no goal in Being, what they express is their longing for rest. It is unendurable, they feel, that Life, creation, change, should travel on their way forever: at the very thought their minds become tired, and Being is conjured up. Hitherto, our goals have not been resting stages, but eternal termini. But a true goal should not be a cul-de-sac, but the peak from which to descry our next goal. And so on eternally? Well, why not? Finality was born when the mind became weary at the thought of eternal ascent and found refuge in that of eternal rest. We have not fully learned yet how to live: struggle is still with us an argument against Life. What we need is perhaps a few re-incarnations! When we have learned to live, however, we shall welcome struggle as a necessary part of Life, and Becoming will be as desirable to us as Being now. And not till then shall we be *fit* for immortality.

164

Love and Sympathy

Love and Hatred are not the true opposites, but Love and Sympathy. Love is creation, that is to say, strife: a battle between the inanimate not yet dead, and the living still unborn. And it is also, therefore, the hatred of the one for the other. True, this hatred may not be of individuals but of things; but does that make it any more harmless? It is naïve democratic prejudice to think that hatred of things is less *wicked* than hatred of individuals; the very opposite is the case! The former is a thousand times more dangerous and destructive than the latter, which, indeed, is little more than an idiosyncrasy. Hatred is contained in and is an aspect of Love; it is Love seen as destruction. Well, only Love has a right to Hatred, for only Love can create.

Sympathy, however, would maintain in existence what should be dead, and would bid what should be living remain forever unborn. For in death and in birth alike there is pain. Sympathy—that is, Sympathy with the *necessary* suffering of existence—is a far greater danger than Hatred.

165

The Humanitarians

Hatred only to things, not to men; Love only to men, not to things: the formula of the half-and-half.

166

Love and the Virtues

Love is the mother of all the harder virtues, and that because she requires them. For how without them could she suffer to create, and endure the pain of Becoming? Everything dynamic must become virtuous. The soft, hedonistic, and degenerate in morality, however, arise from Sympathy. Sympathy needs the comfortable virtues; it seeks the static, for movement is pain, and pain, of the devil—if Sympathy will admit a devil! Its virtues are all in bad training.

167

The Other Side

He ceaselessly groaned that he was weary of life and wished to be rid of it; but all the time it was life that wished to be rid of him.

168

Love and Danger

The fear that danger might perish—the immortal fear of Nietzsche—need cause us no anxiety, could we but believe that creative Love will continue to exist. For Love is the great source of danger, and of the heroic in action and thought. If military wars were to disappear from the earth, danger need not be diminished; it might become emancipated and voluntary: it might be raised from a common necessity to an individual task. Perhaps in the distant future nations will become more pacific, men more war-like; peace will be maintained among nations *in order* that individuals may have a free arena in which to carry on their great contests—"without powder," as Nietzsche said. The battles, born of Love, of the Brands and Zarathustras, not those of the Napoleons: that is what creative Love would envisage! But this prophecy has not sufficient foundation as yet, alas, to be called even a conjecture!

169

Fellowship and Love

Fellowship is of two kinds: that which is inspired by Sympathy, and that which is an expression of Love. Men unite for the mere satisfaction which union brings, or for that which is found in the struggle for more remote things—an aspiration or a vision. This latter thing, impractical and paradoxical, which lends Man what nobility he has—it was Love that gave it to him. Fellowship is the sublime attempt to complete the figure of Man. My friend is he who possesses the qualities which I lack and most need: in that sense, he creates me. Fellowship should enrich *all* who partake of it, make their highest qualities productive, and throw bridges over the chasms of their defects. But the association of men for mere enjoyment is not worthy the name of Friendship. Sympathy is its parent.

170

The Paradox

It is possible to live nobly without Happiness, but not without Love. Love, however, confers the highest happiness. Is it because Love is indifferent to Happiness that Happiness flutters around it, and caresses it with its wings?

171

Moral Indignation

We should altogether eschew moral censoriousness in our contemplation of Life, for it is merely destructive. To destroy that which we cannot re-create in a better form is a crime. Only Love should condemn, for only Love can create. To bring the good into existence, or prepare the way of those who can create the good—that should be our only form of condemnation. In what consists the passion of the moral fanatic? In respect for the law, that it should not be violated. So he would extirpate whatever does not conform, even though thus he should destroy all life, and have no power to create it anew. No wonder he is gloomy: the vulture is not a bird of cheerful mien.

172

Morality and Love

Into what a dilemma falls the poor lover of life who goes to make the choice of morality! He sees that both great types of morality, the humanitarian and the military, the Hedonistic and the Spartan, lead in the end to Nihilism, the one by liquefying, the other by hardening. The former becomes too sensitive to endure Life; the latter, too insensible to feel it. Yet they were to serve Life; but they soon forgot the purpose for which they were formed; they exalted themselves as something higher than Life; they become "absolute," and a stumbling-block to existence. And this was because they were not founded in the beginning upon the very principle of Life, which is Love, but upon accidentals. The conflict between Morality and Love has accordingly been a conflict between the forces of Death and of Life: for "works" without Love are dead. Morality should be but the discipline which Love imposes upon itself in order to create. It should crown all the virtues which oppose a gallant and affirmative countenance to suffering and change, such as heroism, fortitude, joy, temperance. This morality is the antithesis of the humanitarian morality sprung from Sympathy.

173

Paradise Regained

If Life is but an expression of creative Love, then a morality founded upon Love must be the only true morality. And, moreover, in it ethics and the instincts are reconciled; innocence is grasped.

174

Love and Knowledge

If in all Life there is change, creation, Becoming, and if in our lives we know these things only in the interpretation of them which we call Love, must not Love be a necessary part of our knowledge of Life? Observation, investigation and the weighing of results may tell us much *about* Life, and show it to us in many aspects, but it does not give us immediate knowledge. Is it possible to know Life? If Life be the expression of Love——! Upon that "if" depends everything. For if it is justified, then we have within us the clue to the riddle of existence. Perhaps here we discern the faint struggling for birth of that undiscovered faculty of the mind of which men speak. The comprehension of Life through Love! The profoundest of intuitions? The maddest of dreams?

175

Proverb and Commentary

Love is blind, but it is with excess of light.

176

Bad Thoughts

She was as perfect as a drop of dew or a beam of light; a pure thought of God, delicate, spontaneous and finished. There was nothing misshapen in body or soul; Love did well to create such a being. But the others, the crooked, blind and defiled! Are these the bad thoughts of God? From whence do they come? Whither do they go? Conceived in darkness, born for destruction?

177

Love and Sympathy

We must not think of Love as a mere concept. For it is something more real than Life itself: the very Life of Life, the very soul of Becoming. It is a force both spiritual and physical, but transcending the distinction of spiritual and physical. We must not conceive Love as a thing akin to Sympathy. It is not humanitarian or even human; it is a force as unsullied by humanity as the mountain winds or the tides of the ocean. Nevertheless, it is within Man, just as it is within the stars and seas; a great creative, destructive, transforming and purifying force; beyond Good and Evil as the dew and the lightning are. This is the power that is known by Man in his moments of love. He is then free to create and enjoy, as if he were re-born, with a will new, joyful and innocent. But seldom does he attain this knowledge: his moments of exultation are brief. Yet Love has not on that account lost any of its potence. Man may decay and become corrupt; but Love remains unalterable, forever pure, incapable of corruption.

178

Multum in Parvo

You are but a drop in the ocean of Life. True: but it is in the ocean *of Life!*

179

Love and the Senses

When one loves, the distinction between soul and body is passed. In Love alone is the dream of Goethe, Heine, and the moderns realized: here the reconciliation of the spirit and the senses is celebrated in perfect innocence. For Love irradiates and makes fragrant the body in which it dwells, and raises it aloft to sit by its brother the soul.

180

Love and Innocence

Life takes us back to its bosom when we love. The heavens, the earth and the race of men no longer appear things external and hostile, against which we must arm ourselves. We return from exile in personality; our thought sweeps to the farthest horizons, and plunges into the deepest gulfs of existence, at home in all places. The "external" is no longer external: we contemplate it from the inside, we gaze through its eyes. For the very principle of Life, of which all living things are the expression, has been apprehended by us. Our personality has been emancipated. This feeling of universal comprehension is called Innocence.

181

Love and the Fall

Has the fable of the Fall still another interpretation for us? Was the Fall of Man the fall from Love? When the feeling of universal comprehension was lost, personality in the individualistic sense arose. And Sin was the child of this Individualism. To the first man bereft of Love, the earth assumed a terrible mien; nature glared at him with a million baleful eyes: he became an outcast in his home. No longer knowing the earth or other men, he experienced terror, hatred and despair. To protect himself against existence, he created Love's substitute, morality. And with morality arose sin, and perished innocence.

182

Love and its Object

Nietzsche's psychology was wrong when he spoke of Love as a narrowly egoistic thing isolating two people and making them indifferent to every one else. There is too much of the philosopher and too little of the psychologist in this observation. For mankind cannot be loved, Life cannot be loved, until One has been loved. Only lovers can generate such wealth of life that it overflows, enriching their friends, their enemies, all the world. To love one is to love all.

183

Freedom in Love

In true love there is a feeling of entire freedom. Is it because the lovers have by a divine chance found their true path, have become a pulse in the very heart of Life? If Love is the principle of Life, then in Love alone is perfect freedom. Ethics and instinct become one. This is the road that leads beyond good and evil: Man must learn to love.

184

Love and the Sensualists

On those who affirm Life as innocent and holy, there is an obligation laid. Their lives must be innocent: Life must be to them a sustained act of worship. How many of them have been lacking just here! Heine failed, in spite of his real nobility. Goethe, however, attained unity and sincerity; and Nietzsche was a figure of beautiful integrity and innocence. They were neither of them mere "writers." Nor must we be: there is upon us the compulsion to prove that a life of innocence is possible. And as a first step, we must separate ourselves from those who, before they have sought innocence, praise the senses. For they confuse and defile everything.

185

Free Will

Only those who have knowledge of Becoming can know what the freedom of the will is. Freedom—that is to will Becoming with all its suffering, voluntarily to go on the way which Fate and the highest Life direct us. Slavery—that is to deny Becoming, to cling to the static, and to be dragged along the stream of change. To be dragged, not to remain stationary; for men by taking thought cannot gain immunity from change. Their will and their desires avail them nothing. For the stream of Becoming is unchangeable in its power. It is Man that changes. When he affirms Becoming, he is enlarged; when he denies it, he is straitened.

186

Tragedy, Life and Love

In the highest Life two qualities are always to be found together, exuberance and suffering. Life is founded on this paradox, which is fundamental; for in the emotion of Love we are most conscious of it. Love is the most joyful and most suffering thing: its plenitude of joy is so great that it can endure gladly the worst griefs. And tragedy is the truest expression in art of Life and of Love; for its characteristic, too, is a Joy triumphing over Fate.

VI
THE TRAGIC VIEW

187

Life as Expression

Schopenhauer interpreted life as the expression of a Will to Live. Nietzsche showed with profound truth that beneath this will there was something more fundamental, the Will to Power. Have we here got to the foundation, or shall we find that underlying the Will to Power there is something more fundamental still? *Why* do all living things strive for power? Is it, indeed, power that they desire in their striving, power for the sake of power? That which everything by a law of its being searches for is *expression:* the Will to Power is merely an outcome of that search. For seeing that the sun of created Life is split up into individuals, related and yet diverse, the expression of one unit is bound to collide with that of another, and the outcome is a conflict. Life, therefore, is essentially something that injures itself, and injures itself the more the more powerful it is; in a word, Life is essentially tragic. Most people, however, live in illusion, knowing nothing of this. The philosophers, and, before them, the priests, were those who perceived that Life was of this nature; but, alas, from the truth they drew the immediate and not the more profound conclusion. They sought, unconscious Hedonists, a palliative for Life, and contemned expression, which they saw was the cause of suffering. These were the creators of that morality which has prevailed to our own day; a morality antagonistic to Life, anti-tragic, negative. All the systems which have been created in this way are colossal panaceas and remedies: they are not fundamental.

There were others, however, who saw as the priests did that Life was tragic, but who at the same time affirmed it. These were the tragic poets. They were more deeply versed in Life than the priests: tragic art is more profound than morality. For morality is based on the belief that man desires above everything else Happiness. But Tragedy has perceived that this is not so. Man will express himself, it proclaims, whatever the outcome, whether it be joy or suffering.

Since then morality has sunk deep into Life, and there is now almost a second instinct in man striving against expression. Consequently there are many existences passed without expression; sometimes even in a resolute struggle against it, as in the case of innumerable religious men and ascetics. To some men it seems that their spirit has been lying frozen and dead within them, until one day an influence touches them, and they feel an imperious desire to express themselves, to create. This influence is nothing else than Love, which is the desire for expression itself. When its rule is recognized and obeyed Life reaches its highest degree of joy and of pain, and becomes creative. This is the state which is glorified by the tragic poets. To those who affirm, it is the highest condition of Life.

188

"Self-Expression"

Self-expression is something infinitely more subtle than the moderns conceive. This man studied to express himself: he investigated his ego, and thereby cut himself off from Life more completely than any anchorite, for the anchorite had at least heaven in addition to himself. This neo-anchorite, however, turned his eyes deliberately inward and strove to find expression for what he discovered there, but for nothing more. Thus he became his own prison. Eventually he turned out an æsthete.

This other man found that his thoughts and desires flew away from him as irrevocably as a flock of wild birds and became lost or strangers. He seemed constrained to express everything *not* himself, everything foreign, remote and as exalted; but in the end he discovered that it was himself he had expressed. "Thy true being," said Nietzsche, "lies not deeply hidden in thee, but an infinite height above thee, or at least above that which thou dost commonly take to be thyself."

189

Life as a Value

Those who say that the belief in Life as a value is not a belief which will arouse the heroic passions and make men die for it, use a form of reasoning, at any rate, which is erroneous. They first confuse the ideal of more complete existence with the more complete existence of an individual, and then demonstrate that this individual will not lay down his life for the sake of *his* more complete existence! But Life as an ideal is just as impersonal as any other ideal, whether it be Justice or Perfection or Renunciation. True, it has not yet become static, but on that account its attraction is only the stronger; it arouses our very love. And men will die for what they love: they will die for Life.

190

Hebbel's Theory of Tragedy

Hebbel's theory of Tragedy is noble and profound. Not in the misdirection of wills does he find the source of the tragic, but in the core of the will itself, in the inexorable expression and collision of wills. This conception raises Tragedy from a mere consequence and punishment of sin to an expression of Life itself, to the most profound and essential expression of Life. And this is just and worthy of Tragedy. For the character of Tragedy is not negative and condemnatory, but deeply affirmative and joyous. How shallow then must be the theories which would deny Tragedy to the good, to those whose wills are highly directed! Tragedy is not a punishment. The more noble man becomes the more tragic he will also become.

191

Tragic Philosophy

The belief, against which Nietzsche declaimed, that Reason brings Happiness has become to the modern man second nature, so that now the notions of Reason and Happiness are indissolubly connected in his mind. Any argument for a tragic view of Life must therefore appear, first of all, unreasonable; for Happiness as an end is the only reason that will be acknowledged. It remains for us to show that Happiness is itself unreasonable, an impossibility, a chimera. There is no Happiness as an end. Reason does not bring Happiness, nor does virtue, nor does asceticism, nor does comfort. Happiness is an accident. And not even a modern can make accidents happen!

To this modern world, with its belief in Happiness, Nietzsche was bound to appear unreasonable, for he brought with him not only a tragic conception of Life, but a tragic philosophy. A tragic philosophy—the marriage of Knowledge and Tragedy: nothing could have seemed more irrational to modern Europe than that!

192

Tragedy and Arguments

Those who desire to restore a tragic conception of Life should not use these arguments: that Happiness is a condition which, if it were possible of realization, would become intolerable, producing its opposite, unhappiness; or that only when the individual renounces Happiness does Happiness become his. These are the statements of a Hedonism once removed. The argument for the tragic view should be founded on considerations altogether irrelevant to Happiness. It should not care enough about Happiness even to disdain it.

193

Morality and Happiness

Philosophers have from the beginning acknowledged that Happiness is not won by seeking for it, but by striving for other things. This, however, has not prevented them from proclaiming Happiness as the goal of Man and as the deliberate object of ethics. Contradiction upon contradiction! If the individual cannot by taking thought capture Happiness, is it conceivable that a community can, or the human race, in toto? To throw a net round this mirage compounded of desire and fancy—surely Reason was itself the most unreasonable thing to attempt that. And, after all, does Man desire Happiness? Tragedy denies it.

194

End or Effect

One may possess all the virtues save Love, and remain unhappy. Love, however, brings Happiness with it as the sun brings light. Is Happiness, then, the end of morality? Or an effect of Love?

195

Superiority

In order to despise enjoyment, one need only be supremely happy or supremely wretched.

196

Beauty and Tragedy

In every beautiful face there is nobility, strength and a touch of sadness—the seal of tragedy is upon it. To make Life beautiful, then, would be to make it tragic? Nay, rather let us say that to make Life tragic is to make it beautiful. Supreme beauty is but the expression in which are comprised in a miracle of unity the sorrow and the joy of Tragedy. For in the most radiant manifestation of Beauty there is a brooding solemnity; in the most sorrowful there is triumph.

197

Experimenting in Life

The aim of the æsthetes was without enduring Tragedy to enjoy Beauty. To that end they devised their creed of experimentation in Life: they wished to know all the joys of the soul and of the senses without inconvenience to themselves. Perceiving that Love and Beauty bring suffering in their train, they decided to *take the initiative* against them, in other words, to "experience" them. All they experienced, however, was—their experiences. That, indeed, was all they desired: their "experimenting in Life" was escaping from Life. Without the courage to accept Life with the Dionysians or to renounce it with the ascetics, they hit upon the plan of stealing a march upon it. Well, it was certainly not upon Life that they stole a march!

198

Christian and Dionysian

The Christian and the Dionysian are both of them step-children and solutions of Pessimism. A gloomy and realistic view of the world was necessary before either of them could be born. In Christianity Pessimism was translated into symbols. "Original Sin" and "transgression against God"—these were the theological counterparts of the pessimist's "suffering," "the tyranny of the Will." How did Christianity find relief from this fundamental pessimism? By a pathetic illusion in which mankind were transformed into erring children, who, however, were forgiven by an indulgent Father. Here suffering was still an argument against Life, and a palliative was sought and found. The Dionysian, however, affirmed Life in the very tragicality of its aspect, and, by so doing, achieved a victory over it. In short, to the Dionysian Life is a tragedy; to the Christian it is a pathetic tale with a happy ending.

199

History of the Dionysian

In the beginning he possessed innocence: the world appeared to him as beautiful, Man as good, and the future as immeasurable. The great illusion of Rousseau was his—a "natural man" himself, believing in the "natural man," a romanticist, a credulous, not too sincere, "beautiful" soul—a youth with the qualities of youth. But a day came when unwillingly and painfully his soul forced his eyes open and compelled them to look, and he saw without illusion; the cruelty beneath smiling Appearance, the red claw, and conscienceless, inappeasable appetite. Looking at Man he found him a powerless little creature, condemned to a few years in this world, cut off by Death, and even during his life circumscribed by invincible limitation. Nevertheless, this man disdained to hide his head in the sands of illusion; and immediately he became altogether more worthy of respect, more real, almost sublime. A noble resignation to Life now characterized him; the classical writers, especially the Greeks with their naturalistic pessimism, seemed to him the highest thing; and he accepted the theory of Original Sin. All honour to him when he reached, after a painful journey, this spare but real conclusion! All honour to this pessimist who would not deceive himself!

One day, however, the thought came to him, "Even if pain and necessity be the truths of Life! There is something within me which can turn these, also, to account! I can transfigure them. Pain, Struggle, Change—these will no longer enslave me; for these shall be my slaves!" At that moment he became a Dionysian: he had turned the corner of pessimism, and had gained freedom. Original Sin was no longer true for him; for a new truth had dawned in whose light the old was quenched.

From an illusive freedom in the beginning, through bondage to necessity, to a new freedom—the history of the Dionysian. The pessimist is more profound than the "natural man," but the Dionysian is the most profound of all. He burrows deeper than pessimism itself; he grows, the most happy of men, out of the very soil of pessimism.

200

Tragic Affirmation

To feel happy at this moment—is not that to approve of your whole life, of its suffering, conflict, ennui and scepticism no less than its victories and festivals? This moment is what it is by virtue of these experiences; justify it and you justify them. The physical agony which left its mark upon you; the anguish of bereavement and of disillusionment; the cynicism with which you consoled yourself; the years when you lived altogether bereft of hope; your most profound and most petty thoughts and actions; your meanest, bitterest and noblest experiences: all these are unconsciously affirmed in your affirmation of this moment. Let them be affirmed consciously! Or is your soul afraid to go as far as your will? Looking back now with new eyes over your life, you find that precisely what you cannot do is to repent—least of all of your sins and griefs! For to repent is to will Life to be other than Life, and essentially not to affirm.

He who contemplates his life thus, perhaps understands for the first time what is the meaning of Tragedy.

201

Mastery and Tragedy

The desire of Man to subjugate Nature and Fate and obtain mastery over his resources—perhaps it is as well that this is meantime unattainable! For Man's spirit is not yet noble enough for him to use his power aright: he would use it, if he could grasp it now, as a means to Happiness! Our first duty is to fight the idea of Happiness, to make Man tragic. Once Man wills Tragedy, however, the more mastery he acquires the better.

202

The Hidden Faculty

When we speak hopefully of the discovery of still undiscovered faculties in Man, to what do we look forward? In plain terms, how do we expect this faculty to be of use to us? In bringing about Happiness? It is almost a tragedy—it is a tragedy without the nobility—that in our time the most beautiful, heroic and powerful things have to bow their heads and become slaves to this weak and pathetic tyrant, Happiness. Should we then oppose the addition of one more divine power to the imprisoned? Well, a hope consoles us. For the discovery of a new faculty in Man will not make him more happy, but simply more powerful; his self-expression in action will be the more complete; the essential conflict of Life will be magnified; Life will become more tragic. So think well, you votaries of Happiness, before you bring to life another power of the tragic creature, Man. Far better for your ends if you could but succeed in killing some of those he already possesses. But have you not sometimes tried to do that?

203

The Other Side

And yet Man cannot create without Happiness. The soul that lives in shadow becomes unhealthy and sterile: sunshine is after all the great health-bringing and fructifying thing. Happiness does make a man nobler; more ready to generosity and heroism; more careless of enjoyment. Happiness! But what is Happiness? The Happiness that is essential to the best life is a state of the soul: this is doubtless that which Goethe and Heine praised. But the other, the Happiness of the utilitarian, is an effect of calculated action, the reward of a sort of ethical thrift. The first, however, is independent of calculation, and even a little scornful of it; for in its confidence and plenitude it dares to put out on the gloomiest seas. It is not unrelated to Love, this effect of an affirmative attitude to Life. When people praise Happiness, how one desires to believe it is this that they praise.

204

The Two Species

The few have a conception of Life different from that of the many. To the latter still pertain such notions as "do as you would be done by," and so forth. They understand a morality but not the end of morality. The few, however, who understand both the morality and the reason for it, who have a conception of Life more difficult and unyielding, seem to the many cold and a little inhuman. The lives of the latter, on the other hand, appear to the few as a naively happy, narrow and absurd form of existence.

205

Nietzsche

What was Nietzsche, that subtlest of modern riddles? First, a great tragic poet: it was by a divine accident that he was at the same time a profound thinker and the deepest psychologist. But his tragic affirmative was the core of his work, of which thought and analysis were but outgrowths. Without it, his subtlety might have made him another Pascal. The Will to Power, which makes suffering integral in Life; the Order of Rank whereby the bulk of mankind are doomed to slavery; the Superman himself, that most sublime child of Tragedy; and the last affirmation, the Eternal Recurrence: these are the conceptions of a tragic poet. It is, indeed, by virtue of his tragic view of Life that Nietzsche is for us a force of such value. For only by means of it could modern existence, sunk in scepticism, pessimism and the greatest happiness of the greatest number, be re-created.

For the last two centuries Europe has been under the domination of the concept of Happiness as progress. Altruism, the ideology of the greatest happiness of the greatest number, altruism as a means of universalizing Happiness, was preached in the eighteenth century; until after a while it was seen by such clear-sighted observers as Voltaire that men did not obey this imperative of altruism; therefore they were condemned: the moral indignation of the eighteenth century, the century of censoriousness par excellence, was the result. First, an impossible morality was demanded, and for the attainment of an unattainable ideal; then Man was condemned because he failed to comply with it, because he was Man. Thus in the end the ideal of the greatest happiness worked out in pessimism: Life became hideous and, worst of all, immoral, to the utilitarian, when it was seen that altruism and happiness are alike impossible. Schopenhauer is here the heir of Voltaire: the moral condemnation of the one has become in the other a condemnation of Life itself, more profound, more poetical, more logical. Altruism has in Schopenhauer deepened into Pity; for Pity is altruism bereft of the illusion of Happiness.

How was Man to avoid now the almost inevitable bourne of Nihilism? By renouncing altogether Happiness as a value; by restoring a conception of Life in which Happiness was neither a positive nor a negative standard, but something irrelevant, an accident: in short, by setting up a tragic conception of Life. This was the task of Nietzsche: in how far he succeeded how can we yet say?

206

Again

Nietzsche loved not goodness but greatness: the True, the *Great* and the Beautiful. Was not this the necessary corollary of his æsthetic evaluation of Life?

207

Sacrifices

"The first of the first fruits of thy land thou shalt bring into the house of the Lord thy God."

Thus spoke the oldest reverence. We should not scoff at this feeling but rather try to understand it; for it is only too rare in our time. What was its meaning to the rulers of Israel? Gratitude, a beautiful, affirmative thing. To enrich Life with our highest gifts, which we freely offer in thanksgiving for what Life has given us,—that should be our form of sacrifice. And we should perform it gladly, with festive, overflowing heart, not with sullen and conscientious face, as if Life were a usurer.

208

Our Poverty

The spiritual poverty of modern life is appalling; and all the more because men are unconscious of it. Prayer was in former times the channel whereby a profound current of spiritual life flowed into the lives of men and enriched them. This source of wealth has now almost ceased, and Man has become less spiritual, more impoverished. We must seek a new form of prayer. Better not live at all than live without reverence and gratitude! Let our sacramental attitude to Life be our form of prayer. Let us no longer desire to live when that has perished.

Finis

"To abjure half measures and to live resolutely in the Whole, the Full, the Beautiful."—GOETHE.

"To try to see in all things necessity as beauty."—NIETZSCHE.

THE END

Note from the Editor

Odin's Library Classics strives to bring you unedited and unabridged works of classical literature. As such, this is the complete and unabridged version of the original English text unless noted. In some instances, obvious typographical errors have been corrected. This is done to preserve the original text as much as possible. The English language has evolved since the writing and some of the words appear in their original form, or at least the most commonly used form at the time. This is done to protect the original intent of the author. If at any time you are unsure of the meaning of a word, please do your research on the etymology of that word. It is important to preserve the history of the English language.

Taylor Anderson

Printed in Great Britain
by Amazon